D0745829

CALLED TO LIFE

CALLED TO LIFE

Yves Congar

Crossroad New York

1987

The Crossroad Publishing Company
370 Lexington Avenue, New York, N.Y. 10017

Original title: *Appelés à la vie*
© Les Editions du Cerf, 1985

Translated by William Burridge WF

Printed in the United States of America

Library of Congress Cataloging-in-Publication Data

Congar, Yves, 1904–
  Called to life.

  Translation of: Appelés à la vie.
  1. Church. 2. Catholic Church—Liturgy. 3. Holy
Spirit. 4. Revelation. 5. Catholic Church—Doctrines.
  I. Title.
BX1746.C5613 1987   248.3   87-19923
ISBN 0-8245-0835-1

Contents

Introduction

Let God be God
(Fr Congar's prayer)*

Fr Congar would be reluctant to talk about himself. He
has laboured tirelessly, even when ill-health weighed
heavily on him, at his task of theologian at the service of
the Church, the typical Friar Preacher dedicated to the
penetrating study of the faith.

His particular field of investigation has been the
Church, the branch of theology known as ecclesiology.
His approach to it has been thorough and scientific and it
has served to clear the way towards unity between
separated Christian Churches. He has been concerned
especially with the Churches that emerged from the
Reformation and the basis and driving force of his
ecumenism ever since his early years has been the need for
each individual Church to truly know itself and for all the
Churches to acknowledge one another. It was this
perspective that made such an impact on the Second
Vatican Council. It has been a task which involved not
only historical research and erudition but also the
penetrating insight of a man who is a model of love for the
Church and loyalty to it, even in the face of the kind of
jostling to which original thinkers are often exposed.

As long ago as 1967 a bibliography of his books and articles
by Jean-Pierre Jossua, including *Theology for the People of
God*,[1] ran to fifty pages and the list has been growing ever
since. There has been notably in the last few years his three-
volume study titled *I believe in the Holy Spirit*[2].

* *Prier* (April 1981).
1. Chrétiens de tous les temps (Éditions du Cerf).
2. Yves Congar, *I Believe in the Holy Spirit* (Seabury Press/G. Chapman).

The Charismatic Movement — as it is called — has attracted his attention precisely because he sees in it a manifestation of the breath of the Holy Spirit in the Church of today, although it must be said the movement's style of prayer is quite different from his own. "Singing 'alleluia' for an hour-and-a-half on end is not for me," he says, with a twinkle in his eye, "though I am personally convinced that prayer is inseparable from theological study. It is indeed one of its distinguishing facets."

Learning to pray from practice

Yves Congar was born at Sedan in France. He was ten years old when World War One broke out and his childhood was deeply marked by the spectacle of human suffering and death. As a youngster he wanted to be a doctor but he became increasingly attracted to the priestly vocation, inspired by the need in which the world around him stood of remodelling itself, reconverting to Christianity and thus returning to God again. He loves to recall with a touch of humour the fervour with which he and his sister in their ardent preparation for First Communion knocked down the Buddhas their older brothers had made in the sand at the bottom of the garden. Pagan idols could just not be tolerated!

He entered a seminary meaning to become a secular priest and went through the strict "exercises" characteristic of the French seminaries in those days. One prayed for the grace to pray. It was later on, then, that he entered the Dominicans. But in 1919 he had visited a Benedictine monastery and he has never forgotten the impression that glimpse of the monastic life made on him. The monks had been displaced and were living in makeshift quarters. He wrote: "What I saw there was how these monks were living their life of prayer despite the quite unsuitable conditions they found themselves in. It was 6th August and every year I keep the anniversary of that day when I was present there for the First Vespers of the Feast of the Transfiguration. For me that feast has ever since been associated with a turning point in my life."

2

Study and worship

The Liturgy at the Dominican novitiate and at the Friary at Saulchoir where Yves went afterwards was quite distinctly monastic. "I am convinced that there is a marked trait of the monastic spirit in the Dominican vocation. You can see it in the life of St Dominic who was for years a canon regular in Spain, and in the life of Thomas Aquinas who from the age of six to fourteen was a child oblate at Monte Cassino, and it is a strong trait in the life of Father Lacordaire. To lose that trait would, I feel sure, be losing something of our identity as Dominicans.

When I was a young Dominican at Saulchoir, we used to have the Night Office most of the year as well as Lauds, Prime, Terce, Sext, None, Vespers and Compline spread across the day. And our intellectual activities, including the study of theology, was linked with our liturgical prayer. That way it became part and parcel of my life with the deep conviction that that was how it should be and I have always stood by that conviction. The study of theology, in which I have been engaged all my life (except for the seven years when I was in uniform during the last war, part of the time as a prisoner) has always been inseparably linked for me with the celebration of the Liturgy. I find it absolutely essential to 'celebrate' the Mysteries that I am studying. The two are for me one single thing.

The liturgical Office consists essentially of the psalms. They play a major role in my life as indeed they have always done. There is something fantastic in the realisation that from the earliest days the Church has adopted as the vehicle of prayer for priests, religious and laity the psalms, which are the Jewish prayers written at various times between the days of David and the post-exile period, a matter of six or seven centuries. I have rather gone off the psalms expressing imprecation, although it is true that one can give them a spiritual meaning. But if you really want to be absorbed in the psalms you must not allow yourself to be put off by that kind of difficulty: at one and the same time they express prayer and teach us

3

how to pray. They repeat the constant refrain of the People of God, that he is our God whatever the circumstances in which we find ourselves. They may be circumstances in which we experience joy, the sheer joy of living, the joy of reaping a good harvest. But above all there are the wonderful psalms known as the Songs of Ascent or Pilgrimage that sing of the joy of going up to Jerusalem to celebrate the Lord. And this 'going up' does not simply mean setting out from one place to another. It means making a change of heart. It is the utter joy of serving God. 'How lovely is thy dwelling place, Lord God of hosts,' sings Psalm 84, 'One day in thy courts is better than a thousand elsewhere'.

Sometimes however we find ourselves in circumstances that bring distress. For this there are the psalms that declare one's hope and plead for help: 'For thee, O Lord, do I wait, it is thou, O Lord, who will answer'. Then come those surprising psalms of David as he flees from Saul, psalms full of anguish and yet crying out their trust in God.

Or again there is the well known Psalm 21. It was the first verse of this psalm that Jesus himself pronounced on the Cross: 'My God, my God, why hast thou forsaken me?' — that messianic psalm which, I think, Christ must have recited in its entirety on the cross, at least mentally. Then again there is Psalm 119 where each verse makes an allusion to God's design, his divine will and his law which is not to be interpreted in a legalistic frame of mind but in a theological perspective. It is rather like a kaleidoscope where the picture is always changing and yet is always the selfsame thing. The psalm expresses the life of union with God, and throughout there is the constant reassurance that the Lord is my God whatever may befall me.

On a banner displayed one day at a meeting of the World Council of Churches were the words: 'Let God be God'. I find that impressive. It points straight to the heart of prayer, for to pray means making that statement a reality in our lives. Of course, God is God whether or not we are conscious of him. But we can be instrumental in assuring that he is God in us, in others and in society at large. Underlying that statement is the great question as to, how there can be other beings outside the very Being himself. The answer is: only by participation in his being. Prayer is a recognition of that fact.

By praying we acknowledge the sovereignty of God and our dependence on him. In point of fact, who are we? What does human life really amount to in the vast cosmos? Why in the face of billions of stars and galaxies should there be this breath that animates the human being? A breath of life and consciousness. Creatures dependent on God and yet created in his image and likeness. Prayer is before all else a gift of God to us, for he knows us before we ever come to know him. He precedes us.

But there is always the temptation for us to usurp the place of God in our regard, that God may not be our God. We have it in our power either to withdraw from God or behave in such a way that he is our God.

In an ecumenical translation of the Our Father the words 'hallowed be thy name' are rendered, 'may you be acknowledged as God'. It is not a literal translation but it does give the exact meaning of the petition. Our Christian prayer is a prayer that the Father may thus be Father and invokes him with that affection and familiarity enshrined in the expression Jesus himself used: 'Abba! Father!'

We do not know exactly what Jesus' prayer was like but there are two or three passages in the Gospel that give us a glimpse of it. We suddenly hear him say, 'Father, I give thanks for thou hast heard my prayer'. And in the exaltation of the Holy Spirit he exclaims: 'Father, I give thee thanks that thou hast hidden these things from the wise and understanding and revealed them to babes'. The human prayer of Jesus was clearly prayer addressed to the Father. And we have a further echo of it in the agony in the Garden: 'Not my will but thine be done' ".

Uniting ourselves with God's will

"It is the liturgical prayer that provides me with the essential axis of my life. Private personal prayer can take on all sorts of forms. There are for instance the ejaculatory prayers, a word or two 'tossed up', as the word implies, to God as we go about our various occupations, directing us straight up to God from the world that lies around us.

Another form is meditation based on the Sacred Scriptures and mental prayer by which we place our whole being in the presence of God. There are different styles of mental prayer to suit different vocations and the varying spiritual needs of individuals and types of spiritual experience.

For some people it will be a meditation full of ideas, for others it will be purely affective prayer. Personally I go rather for the affective type because I find that mental prayer means essentially uniting myself with the will of God. Prayer has often been defined as lifting up the mind and heart to God. St Augustine points out that this entails modifying our will. We draw near to God when we master our will and unite it with the will of God. Of course we are always having distractions in our mental prayer and our mind goes wandering all over the place. What we have to do, I find, is to harness our distractions to our prayer. My thoughts go off to somewhere where I have been, something that has happened to me or something I shall shortly be doing. Why not turn those thoughts into prayer? We can pray for the people and things that crop up in our distractions.

Charles de Foucauld, the modern hermit in the Sahara, said that prayer means thinking lovingly of God. That is a truly simple statement and it says everything. The basis of prayer is indeed the love of God. Prayer must always be made up of thinking lovingly of God and lovingly uniting our will with his.

Prayer of petition follows the same pattern. You find this in the Old Testament, in the Gospel and in the entire experience of the Church. By and large when we have prayed for something things go on as before and our prayers do not seem to have been answered at all. But time and again God does intervene. You can see it in the Bible. It occurs in the lives of ordinary Christians. It even goes to the length of producing miraculous interventions —

6

granted, however, that there are big and little miracles. In the Charismatic Movement there are some cures, even physical ones, that are fairly impressive. But, once more, events just run their usual course.

I would place the prayer of petition at two different levels. I have found the first of these in Père Sève's little book[3] which many people have found helpful because it is down to earth and does not theorise but offers practical hints. He explains that the prayer of petition enables us to match up to the particular situation in which we find ourselves. But there is another dimension and, we note, the two levels are complementary. It lines up with the text of St Paul in the Letter to the Romans, Chapter 8, where he says we do not know how to pray as we ought but that the Spirit himself intercedes for us and he knows what is in keeping with the will of God. All in all the prayer of petition means desiring what God himself desires. It spells total trust, the cry 'Let God be God' taken unreservedly, sometimes even heroically. For it may mean we have to face up to situations with which our human resources left to themselves cannot possibly cope.

The part played by the Holy Spirit in prayer is indispensable. It is the Spirit who fosters in us the filial appeal to God. And thus there is nurtured in our soul, conscious as we are of our own powerlessness, the desire that God himself may dwell in us as our peace, our joy, our activity and our prayer. A passage written by William of Saint-Thierry, friend and correspondent of St Bernard, away back in the twelfth century, works out the idea that the love with which God loves becomes the love with which we love.

All this needs to be carefully thought out. On the face of it, it might be said, if it is the Holy Spirit who prays in us then it is not really our own prayer. Or does it mean he prays through us? The answer is that we must see the Holy Spirit dwelling in us, suscitating prayer in us and being himself the mould of that prayer. By his presence in us he moulds our prayer to his own image and transforms us in such a way that we desire God with God's own desire.''

3. André Sève, *Trente minutes pour Dieu* (Éditions du Centurion).

Prayer for unity

We have said that for Fr Congar prayer is a distinctive facet of theology. And this holds true, as we may well suspect, for the long and patient labours to draw separated Christians together towards unity, in other words the ecumenical initiatives which have been Yves Congar's great life-long mission.

"Prayer for unity is *par excellence* the prayer of Jesus, his 'priestly prayer' (cf. Jn 17). From the day of my ordination in July 1930, whenever I could and the liturgical rubrics allowed, I said the Votive Mass for Unity. It is a beautiful Mass and the Gospel is precisely that prayer of Jesus in St John. And that prayer itself has played a major role in my life. A priest has sacramental power and as a priest I can say: 'This is my body', although it is not *my* body but the Body of Christ; so also in saying 'Father, that they may be one as we are one', I am making present the prayer of Jesus, the prayer he once said on a given day . . . I voice that petition in his very own prayer. He voiced it in this selfsame prayer which is my very own.

In the years I refer to, the only prayer recited together in ecumenical meetings was the Our Father. Nowadays we pray much more together. Of course, we are not yet one and there is still a long way to go, but we have certainly drawn impressively closer together.

This prayer, as we have just said, brings into operation Christ's own prayer, as though in an anticipated fulfilment. We might compare it with Isaiah's prophetic pronouncement, 'the Spirit of God is upon me . . . he has sent me', which Jesus was one day to read in the synagogue at Nazareth, adding 'Today this Scripture has been fulfilled in your hearing'.

Praying also entails talking to God by means of those everlasting prayers, the Our Father, the *Gloria in excelsis Deo*, the *Magnificat*. I never tire of using the *Magnificat*. It is a prayer of hope and security as well as of thanksgiving. I sing it every day at Vespers but I have also made a habit of using it, at least at major festivals, as a prayer of Mary and of the Church. I find that it strikes a chord in a truly remarkable way.

I am also strongly attracted to prayers of intercession that present a kind of struggle with God in prayer, like the prayer of Abraham interceding for the people of Sodom. Intercession is an intervention in order to plead with God on behalf of other people or for the whole world, a pleading which has been described as diverting his justice and drawing down his mercy. It is presented through the intermediary of Christ, for, as I have had occasion to point out to the Charismatic Movement, there is no Breath without the Word and no Word without the Breath. The imagery of breath and spoken word is very apt. Without the use of breath a word remains unspoken and it is by the Holy Spirit that the Word is uttered."

The tale of the cherry tree

Despite his poor health Fr Congar has carried steadily on with his work. Surely he has been enabled to do so thanks to the Holy Spirit who brings about the union of our will with the will of God.

"Things are what they are; that is all there is to it. Other people have been more severely tried than me. I remember in our garden at home we had a cherry tree. One day it was struck by lightning and almost all its branches were destroyed. But one branch was left hanging on by a thread. And do you know, that branch went on producing cherries. We have to take stock of the potentials we are left with. A time may come when we shall be left with nothing at all! But generally speaking there is enough left to be happy about and to keep life going and get some work done."

Whatever would my prayer be without the prayer of others?

Year in year out a religious prays every day side by side in the company of other members of the community. What does this add up to? Does it help the person to pray?

9

"Without a doubt it does, but it does not stop at the community; it includes all fellow Christians — Catholic, Protestant, Orthodox — all have been a great help to me. They help to keep me up to the mark. So do the members of a women's group I look after. Fervent souls they are; some of them lead a life of deep faith and love of God and of prayer and charity.

Almost every evening I invoke a dozen or so of my fellow Dominicans who I believe to be very close to God: all our forerunners. I often ask myself what my prayer or even my faith would be worth without the faith and prayer of others. We are of course made for one another. My prayer involves the Communion of Saints: Augustine, Basil, Paul, Abraham, David. They are a factor in my prayer and I am indebted to their help."

(The above reflections were compiled by Janine Feller)

Chapter 1

The psalms in my life*

Many people who genuinely want to pray just cannot get on with the psalms. There are so many allusions in them that mean nothing to them and religious exhortations which no longer register. Quite simply the psalms belong to a type of literature and culture and religious setting of long ago, all so different from ours. It comes as a surprise to realise that the Christian Church from the very first has held on to the psalms as a medium for prayer. The Fathers of the Church wrote commentaries on them. They were used as books to learn to read from for hundreds of years. Passages from them are woven into the Liturgy. They are relied on as a means of sanctifying the day in the Divine Office for monks, nuns and priests and a good number of lay people too.

It may seem strange that Christians should have adopted this specifically Jewish literature for the purposes of prayer. But really they could never have done so unless one way or another there was some connection between that literature and Christ. After all, did not Jesus Christ himself say that the Scriptures and in particular the psalms made references to him? (cf. 24,27.44–46; Jn 5,39.46) And did not the Apostles, in advance of the Fathers of the Church and the early Christians, detect the story of Christ indicated in the Jewish Scriptures? (cf. Jn 1,45; 22,22; 12,16.41; 19,28; 20,9). Come to think of it, the Jews themselves in the course of Old Testament times came to see new perspectives as they went over the history and their Scriptures again and again. That is what they did with the

* *La Vie Spirituelle* (November – December 1975).

11

psalms when they returned from the Exile which sparked off for them newly-kindled hopes of liberation and salvation in the midst of new conditions of poverty and weakness and the novelty of being involved in the history of the world at large with messianic and eschatological hope. Not surprising then that Christians in their turn gave a Christian cast to the psalms and found a kind of Christology in them. The psalter, said St Hilary, is as it were the body of Christ through which the prophet speaks and sings. This Christology of the psalms has been the object of close and detailed study. It follows two lines of approach which sometimes coincide. The first is to attribute to Christ the quality of "Lord". This is facilitated by the fact that the Hebrew word *Yahweh* (God) is rendered *Kyrios* in the Greek Septuagint Bible and *Dominus* in the Latin Vulgate. Besides this, throughout the New Testament the attributes of monotheism are transferred to Christ. In this aspect of the psalter the psalms are seen as addressed to Christ or as praising the virtues and actions associated with him. The other line of approach is seen in the psalms as prayers said by Christ. It is he who is praising God. It is he above all who is the Suffering Servant uttering his anguished supplication. The Letter to the Hebrews bears this interpretation out (cf. 5,7) and so do the Gospels themselves as the record of the cry of Jesus on the cross (cf. Ps 22,2): "My God, my God, why hast thou forsaken me?"

St Augustine thought it was not possible to attribute to Christ himself that sort of sense of being abandoned nor such sentiments as a sadness and anguish. If such words, traced back to the psalms, were attributed to him they must be understood as being uttered by Christ in the name of his Body, that is to say of all Christians.

This Christological aspect of the psalms is too solidly supported by the Fathers and the Liturgy not to justify its use as a key to praying the psalter. All the same, I personally feel no need for this aspect and apart from the instances found in the liturgical texts do not pursue it.

But the psalms do indeed bring us a wealth of

fulfilment, a sense of security and reassurance and an interior sense of peace.

It is too little to say, as did Stalin's daughter Svetlana who was brought to the brink of baptism: "Nowhere have I found more impressive wording than in the psalms. This ardent poetry purifies, strengthens, gives rise to hope in the moments of greatest stress. It forces one to examine oneself, pass judgement on oneself and wash away with tears the waywardness of one's heart. It is an inexhaustible fire of love and gratitude, humility and truth".

The psalms are the very breath of my soul, its spontaneous, joyous self-expression. In the psalms I find myself in a friendly, homely atmosphere, part and parcel of my spiritual life.

The right language for speaking to God

By their sheer literary quality, and something far beyond that alone, the psalms provide the expression of our faith in the living God. The use we make of them owes its value to the degree of our faith in the God of the Bible in terms of unhindered love of him and of our grasp of what he truly is. God is portrayed in the Bible as both creator and redeemer. The mighty deeds of God proclaimed in the psalms concern either creation or liberation and the story of salvation. There are psalms that deal with one or the other and sometimes both are found together. What is most characteristic about the living God is that he is always spoken of as one engaged in action. He is always, for example, the God who forgives sins, cures the sick, rescues from the abyss, bestows grace, brings complete happiness, enacts justice, and so on.

God is basically "he who brought Israel out of Egypt". The psalms often recall this historical event as they praise God and affirm hope in him (cf. Pss 105, 106, 107, 114, 135, 136). The word *Yahweh*, which occurs 670 times in the psalter — to which must be added the word *Elohim* which replaces it in Psalms 42 to 83 — means the living God. To translate it by "the Lord" is to lose its most significant overtones. According to the best interpretation

13

of God's revelation to Moses (cf. Ex 3,14), it means: "I am present" with you; "I shall be who shall be", as you will see from what I do on your behalf. Yahweh does not so much signify "he who is", "the eternal one" — though that aspect must not be lost sight of — as the living God who chooses, calls, consecrates a particular nation for himself, watches over it, guides, chastises it and pardons it. In a word, it means God seen as the author of the economy of salvation. That, then, is God as we must meet him in the psalms. And praying the psalms consists in saying to him with all the distress or joy and cries for help and words of thanksgiving which current circumstances may elicit: "You are my God, you will always be my God".

It has long been the custom to follow the biblical scholar Hermann Gunkel (1926) in grouping the psalms under such headings as hymns, plaintive petitions, supplications by individuals or groups or nations, royal psalms, wisdom psalms and so on. The leading commentator to date, H. J. Kraus, does this, and other authors adopt something of the same kind of classification. This is useful if you want to study the psalms as literature or pick out the various themes they contain, but it does not help much when it comes to absorbing the religious genius of the psalms, for that is of a theological character. Here we have to see the psalms in the light of a deep and vivid understanding of the One to whom they are addressed. The grouping of the psalms by Gunkel and others only gives the various settings — sometimes using imagery, like the ten-chord lyre in Psalm 92,4 or Psalm 144,9, in which the religious soul declares, "You are my God, you will always be my God". They may be doing it in the joy of going up to Jerusalem for the great festivals or in the happy serenity of faithfully serving God (cf. Pss 84 and 122), in the sheer satisfaction of observing the Law (cf. the superb Ps 119). It may be in joining in the praise expressed in liturgical rites which re-create, as our own liturgies do, God's interventions on behalf of his people or of his creation at large. Take for instance Psalm 136: "Give thanks to the Lord for he is good, for his steadfast love endures for ever. . .

14

It is he who remembered us in our low estate, for his steadfast love endures for ever. . . He gives food to all flesh, for his steadfast love endures for ever". We are here brought into the liturgical role of the psalms, their link with worship and their function as "memorial", thanks to which each successive generation can relive the saving acts of God.

There will be times when we are distressed or ill (cf. Pss 38 and 41) or victims of injustice (cf. Ps 109,31). We will find ourselves in the company of David hunted down and fleeing from Saul or from Absalom (cf. Pss 3; 54; 57; 59; 142; 143) or plunged in a sense of being totally abandoned (cf. Ps 88). We cry out for help and find prayers we need in the unforgettable supplications in a dozen or more psalms. We will find ourselves in the company of the *anawim*, the poor of Yahweh, the people who look to him for support. And the answer to our prayer will come from him who "remembered us in our low estate and rescued us from our foes. . ." (Ps 136,23–24). "The Lord is near to the broken-hearted and saves the crushed in spirit" (Ps 34,18). "I thank thee for thou hast answered me and hast become my salvation" (Ps 118,21). The Israelite portrayed in the Bible offers us a model of what every religious person living by that selfsame faith in Yahweh should be. It is in the historical setting and in circumstances that cannot always easily be pinned down precisely, that the person is led to exclaim: "You are my God". It is, again, that same cry rooted in sound doctrine, which we find in the psalms and which we make out own in joy or pain, in supplication or praise. Lastly we note that supplication itself turns into praise. That is the religious outlook of David. That is why he can be thought of as the mastermind of the Book of Psalms even though it turns out that only a small number of the psalms were textually composed by him. We find the same outlook in the great prophets. There are echoes of it in the tender-hearted Jeremiah and in the unknown genius who wrote Parts II and III of the Book of Isaiah.

Some people are put off by the psalms cast in the mould of imprecation and revenge. But these psalms too have to be seen as it were from God's outlook: they are a call for justice and protection addressed explicitly to him. True enough, the kind of ills these psalms looked for are typical of a literary genre belonging to a particular and long since outdated environment. They find their equivalent in the vocabulary still used by certain peoples today. These psalms must be read in the perspective of militancy against the enemies of the Kingdom of God who are very real. These psalms are also rooted in sound doctrine. They belong to the biblical perspective which sees two radically opposed areas of action, God on the one hand and Satan on the other. This, by the way, does not imply any departure from monotheism which is supreme in the Bible. If there is any dualism in the context it is not metaphysical but ethical and, in that sense, existential.

People may be put off by some other types of psalms as well. There may be some which, if one forgets the general ethos of the psalter in reading them, seem incompatible with genuine spiritual experience. One needs a good Scripture commentary when reading them. But it is much simpler just not to make too heavy-going of them and to keep them, if indeed there really are such psalms, in the resounding refrain of the psalter: "You are my God".

"*My* God". This wonderful expression is for ever recurring in the psalms. It does not simply, as do some more ancient narratives, that "my" is asserting that he is not the God of some other nation or clan. What "my" does in the psalms is to point to the union that exists between Yahweh and his people and faithful followers, established by the choice of them and alliance with them made by God. It signifies, as it does in the Prophets, that this is God in whom one has rooted one's faith, whom one invokes with complete confidence and whom one praises with heartfelt joy. "My God" is indeed an ejaculation that springs from the heart.

Quite apart from this invocation there are some eighty psalms where the first person singular, "I", is used. There has been considerable discussion among Scripture scholars as to whether this is meant to designate an individual who is speaking or a group thinking of itself as a personality.

16

Seen that way the discussion is fairly futile. The "I" of these psalms is meant to be a person who embodies all that Israel stands for. We might spell it out like this. It can be someone who lives out and portrays the relationship of faith and praise with the living God. It can be the author of the psalm, the person reciting it, I myself putting the prayer into practice, the community of the faithful, all of us together, the Church as a body, Christ himself (cf. Mt 26,30). *In multis unus*, one in many, said St Augustine. But we could turn that round the other way as *multi in uno*, many in one, in keeping with Augustine's quotation of Psalm 119,63: "I am a companion of all who fear thee". In Christian theology it is the Holy Spirit who unites all those who invoke God. He actualises the prayer he has inspired, whether in the heart of the individual praying alone or in the faithful community, in the prayer of the pious Israelite or in the prayer of the Church which is the Body of Christ.

Praying the psalms as a Christian

As we have already noted, people are sometimes surprised that the psalms should have become the prayer of Christians and even of the public worship of the Church. Several explanations of this have been put forward. Some scholars argue from the fact that unity of the People of God, first found in Israel, was projected into the Church. Then again the notions of Kingdom, Messiah, sacrifice are a key to the link between the two Testaments or two Dispensations. For scholars who make a point of the Christology of the psalms it is precisely the reference they contain to Christ that provides a basis for the passage from Israel to Christianity and nurtures it. Personally I do not find any real need to argue along those lines. All that is needed is that we find clear evidence in the Old Covenant of relationship to God rooted in a living faith. There is plenty of evidence of that and of the fact that the psalms afford a perfect medium for imparting that religious outlook and fostering it.

That Old Testament outlook already bears the stamp of

17

Christianity by the sheer fact that it rings true. The theology of the faith presented in the Letter to the Hebrews is quite simply the history of the patriarchs. In the Old Testament the psalms offer the most profound and sensitively presented religious values. This is so true that Père Evode Beauchamp[1] and Père Jean-Pascal de Relles have written a commentary of the psalms laid out in the framework of the invocations and petitions that make up the Our Father. Of course, in the light of the New Testament we henceforth invoke God as Father in a different sense from that envisaged when the title was associated with Yahweh in the Old Covenant. The Christian invocation takes over the substance of the religious outlook expressed in the Jewish psalms but adds much more to it.

"Make yourself known as God" (Mt 6,9), "Let God indeed be God": such is the constant theme of the psalms as they praise God, tell of his works, implore his help.

It must, however, be affirmed that the relationship to God is henceforth accomplished in Christ through the Holy Spirit. It is as Christians that we make the psalms our prayer. That calls for a certain Christianising of them. Our treasured inheritance of Tradition and the Fathers of the Church and our fervour in the Liturgy all awaken our awareness. But it must be said that we are here thinking especially of our *daily* recitation of the psalms in the Divine Office (the Prayer of the Church) and in personal prayer, whereas the classical application of Christology is mainly concerned with the celebration of the mysteries of Christ. When we use the psalms as prayer it is above all to find in them the relationship of our lives to God in terms of our own spiritual worship, as we read in Romans 12,1, presenting ourselves as a living sacrifice holy and acceptable to God, which is our spiritual worship. But it is through Jesus Christ that our spiritual sacrifices are acceptable to God (cf. 1 Pt 2,5). Given that the psalms express our religious dimension, that is to say the "*ad Deum*" (orientation to God) of our whole life and the life

1. Évode Beauchamp. *Israel en prière. Des psaumes au Notre Père* (Cerf 1985).

18

of the People of God, then it follows that this orientation must be given a genuine Christian cast.

God has revealed himself in Jesus Christ. The "I am who I am" of Exodus 3,14 is transformed into "I am the bread of life" (Jn 8,35), the "light of the world" (Jn 8,12), "the gate of the sheepfold", "the good shepherd" (cf. Jn 10,7–11), "the resurrection" (Jn 11,25), "the way, the truth and the life" (Jn 14,6), "the vine" (Jn 15,1). (These are the famous "I am" of the Gospel of John.) The "I shall be with you" of Exodus 3,12 is clearly pinpointed by "I am with you always to the close of the age" of Matthew 28,20. The name one must invoke in order to be saved (cf. Joel 3,5) is the name of Jesus (cf. Rom 10,13; Acts 2,21). To God's decree, "To me every knee shall bow" (Is 45,23) we must add, "Therefore God has highly exalted him . . . that at the name of Jesus every knee should bow in heaven and on earth and under the earth", from the hymn in praise of Christ in Philippians 2,9–10. And this brings an adjustment to the relationship of God as seen in the Old Testament. The relationship is now effected through God humbling himself to come to us in the form of Servant. It follows that praying the psalms as disciples of Christ, members of his Body, with all that it means to be a Christian, is clearly not praying in quite the same way as the Jews used to do. Certain new shades of meaning came in with the translations first from Hebrew into the Greek of the Septuagint and then into the Latin of the Vulgate. That does not mean that the language was toned down in any way. The overtones are adjusted to ensure that the text conveys the truths contained in it, reflecting how we fit into the full reality of the life of the People of God, a life that enshrines hope, Israel's unshakeable trust, the cry for help in the midst of trials, the humility and mercy accomplished in Christ, his love and that perfect obedience in which he found his glory.

The psalms mean so much to me. They are the daily bread that nurtures my hope, they give voice to my service of God and my love of him. Would that I could penetrate all the wealth they contain as my lips shape their words. They never grow out of date, their content is never exhausted. They take up all the experience of our human life and make us see it in the light of faith. If the psalms play this pervasive role in my life it is because they unfold it all in the presence of God. As we recite the psalms they refreshen our heart and our lips as only truth can. Two words may sum up all that the praying of the psalms means to me. The first is that word of personal commitment to all that has gone before: Amen. And the second follows spontaneously in its wake: Alleluia! Praise be to God!

Chapter 2

Listening and seeing[*]

There are two basic notions in the Old Testament, "to believe" and "to obey". But Hebrew is a language that uses the imagery of action and so "to believe" is expressed as "taking one's stand on" and "to obey" as "to give ear to". Interestingly the Latin word *"oboedire"* (to obey) comes from *"audio"* (I hear), so that obedience is defined as the act of listening. The account of Yahweh's rejection of Saul (cf. 1 Sam 15) illustrates this. Saul, after victory, ought to have slaughtered the animals he had taken as booty. He did not do so and he pretended he had kept them to offer as a ritual sacrifice. Samuel took him to task and said: "Has the Lord as great delight in burnt offerings and sacrifice as in obeying (literally, "harkening to") the voice ("the words of") Yahweh? Behold, to obey ("listening") is better than sacrifice and to harken than the fat of rams" (1 Sam 15,22; cf. Amos 5,21–25; Hos 6,6; Mt 9,13 and 12,7).

"Hear, O Israel"

It is significant that Jewish piety was anchored in the recitation of the famous *Shema Israel*, "Hear, O Israel", taken from Deuteronomy 6,4–9 (cf. also Deut 11,13–31; Num 15,37–41). What this solemn admonition set out was nothing less than the fundamental condition on which their entitlement to being the People of God depended, namely, to harken to God with submission, which is nothing other than an act of faith. It is spelt out in Jeremiah where God says: "This command I gave them,

* *La Vie Spirituelle* (May 1969).

'obey my voice and I will be your God and you shall be my people' " (Jer 7,23 and 14,4; cf. Is 55,3). And in Exodus 19,5–6 we read: "Therefore if you will obey my voice and keep my covenant you shall be my own possession among all peoples; for all the earth is mine and you shall be to me a kingdom of priests and a holy nation". Through and through the alliance is knit together by this fundamental listening, believing and obeying. It is there that you find the key to the entire history of Abraham, "the man of faith", which is the starting point of the history of the People of God, that holy, consecrated nation of which, in the fulness of time, Christ will make himself the Head. It was to good purpose that the ancients called Abraham "the father of (the entire) Church" and that the elect are spoken of as received into "Abraham's bosom".

It is in that age-long history that we must see ourselves, in that long caravan marching steadily towards its promised land with the Prophets and the Apostles as its guides and pacemakers. That indeed is their role, for it was to them that the word of the Lord was first spoken and it is through them that it comes to us. Chosen to be the first to hear it they in their turn exclaimed: "Hear, O heavens and give ear, O earth, for the Lord has spoken" (Is 1,2; cf. also Is 1,10; Jer 2,4; Amos 7,16). The severest reproach they can make to anyone is that of wilfully refusing to listen (Jer 7,13; Hos 9,17; cf. also Is 65,2).

The word of the Lord is not meant just to communicate information with no practical consequence either for him or for the person receiving it. It is productive and it demands a response. That is why this "harkening" is not simply "being well informed" but demands obedience. This presupposes a heart ready to respond, a heart attuned to "seeking God" (cf. Jer 29,13), prepared to go wherever he may call us and to whatever he expects of us even if it goes against the grain. That is why in the Gospels Jesus distinguished between the way the true disciple hears the word of God and the shallow disinterestedness of the casual listener, the kind of people described in Jeremiah 5,21 as foolish and senseless people. There are ears which really grasp what they hear and others for whom words convey nothing. Jesus has a parable about it. The good seed is sown on stoney ground, among thorns and on good soil (Mk 4,3–12 and 8,18; cf. also Is 6,9–10; Ezek 12,2). To hear the word of God and accept it means carrying out the commandments it contains (cf. Lev 18,4; Deut 4,1–6; Lk 8,15; Mt 28,20; Jn 8,55 and 14,24). Whoever hears the word and puts it into practice builds a house on a rock foundation (cf. Mt 7,24f). "It is not hearers of the law who are righteous before God but the doers of the law who will be justified" (Rom 2,13).

Jews and Greeks: hearing and sight

Thus, then, from beginning to end the People of God is characterised and constituted by virtue of hearing the word and accepting it with active faith. It would be almost a platitude to state that the Jewish people, the people of the Bible, is characterised by hearing, whilst the Greeks, to whom we trace the beginnings of the arts and our culture, are characterised by the use of sight. No one is likely to challenge that statement. It is borne out by the terminology employed to express the relationship of believers to their God. The verb "to hear" appears 1100 times in the Old Testament: the God of the Bible is the God who speaks. Even the divine apparitions, the theophanies, in the Old Testament and in particular in the written prophecies, are brought to a head not by the vision itself but by the message they convey and the spoken word. Their purpose is to intensify and give greater impact to God's intervention and his presence. The quite unique episode of the burning bush (Ex 3) is a striking instance of this. Moses begins approaching the bush to *see* what it can possibly be, but the only enlightenment he gets is through his *hearing*. Indeed he veils his face for fear that his eyes might rest on God, for "no man can see his face and live". Seeing God is to come at the end of time. It belongs to eschatology and will bring history to a close. "The Lord", Exodus tells us, "used to speak to Moses as a man speaks to his friend" (Ex 33,11; cf. Num 12,8) but for all that he tells Moses: "You shall see my back, but my face shall not be seen" (Ex 33,23). A rabbinical midrash speaks of the possibility of Moses having "seen the word of the Lord" but nothing more.

Now the Greek religion was clearly a visual religion. To begin with, for the Greeks sight is the best of all the senses. They have a point there, and Thomas Aquinas backs it as regards things that are humanly recognisable objects. In the matter of religious experience sight plays a decisive role. The evidence of this is found especially in connection with the mystery religions which, it is true, are not the most ancient forms of religion. But the most ancient mythology thrives on manifestations of the gods in a visible human form. Israel, by way of contrast, came to understand that far from devising an image of God in our human likeness we must let ourselves be moulded by God. In Israel making of an image of God was banned and was sheer idolatry. Significantly the word "idol", *eidolos*, comes from *eidos* which means external aspect, shape, appearance.

The New Testament, era of the Word made flesh

It might be taken for granted that the emphasis must have shifted from hearing to seeing by the fact of the Incarnation. It is true that it is the Word who becomes incarnate and that focuses on hearing. "In many and various ways God spoke of old to our fathers by the prophets; but in these last days he has spoken to us by a Son" (Heb 1,1–2). But, on the other hand, in Jesus Christ God the Father manifests himself: he took flesh, made himself visible. "Philip, he who has seen me has seen the Father" (Jn 14,9; cf. also 1,18). Or as the Preface for Christmas puts it: "In him we see our God made visible". That is undeniably the all-important fact. But an examination of the New Testament throws further light on the subject. It uses the verb "to see" 680 times whereas it uses "to hear" 425 times. The use of "to see" is specially in evidence in St John. True enough it is John who records the episode of Thomas' momentary incredulity and the concluding remark which concerns us Christians in the post-apostolic age: "Have you believed because you have seen me? Blessed are those who have not seen yet believe" (Jn 20,29). But John is also "the visionary of Patmos" and his Book of Revelation is full of his visions, and its opening chapter even contains these significant words: "Then I turned *to see* the voice that was speaking to me" (Rev 1,12).

However, faith is the operative factor throughout the New Testament and faith comes from hearing the Word (cf. Rom 10,14: "How are they to believe in him of whom they have never heard"). Alongside the trait we have just noted in St John we could pick out instances of just the opposite. Look for example at the way St Luke, for all his use of Greek, tells about Jesus' intervention in the synagogue at Nazareth. After having read from Isaiah the passage about the Messiah, Jesus sits down and declares: "Today this scripture has been fulfilled in your hearing" (Lk 4,21). We would have expected "in your sight". Then again, if there ever was an instance where the Lord manifests himself as visible, even as light, it is at the Transfiguration, an incident of impenetrable meaning. It is clearly a vision. And yet it ends with these words: "This is my beloved Son with whom I am well pleased; listen to him" (Mt 17,5).

The Apostles both heard and saw. "Blessed are your eyes, for they see, and your ears, for they hear" (Mt 13,16; Lk 10,23–24). "That which we have heard, which we have seen with our eyes. . .", St John was to say (1 Jn 1,1). Both seeing and hearing form part of the Revelation to which the Apostles have to bear witness. For that Revelation was not brought about by the spoken word alone even if that appears to predominate (cf. Heb 2,3). It is clear that seeing was a medium of Revelation, seeing the signs and works of Christ, seeing him on the cross and afterwards alive, to have seen him at prayer (cf. Lk 11,1) and breaking bread (cf. Lk 24,31). This is why Vatican II in its Constitution on Divine Revelation says that this economy of Revelation is realised by deeds and words which are intrinsically bound up with one another. However, after the Apostles, the Church, founded on them, is formed by faith given by

God through the intermediary of their witness. Thus, although seeing is not totally excluded, hearing assumes the key role again, hearing, that is, as the equivalent of obeying. St Paul praises the people he is writing to for their faith (cf. Rom 1,8; 1 Thess 1,8) and later he speaks of the obedience of faith (cf. Rom 1,5; 16,26; 2 Cor 10,5–6), an expression bursting with meaning which, incidentally, the Councils of the Church have made use of in their teaching on the nature of faith. Sacred Scripture's most explicit explanation of faith, chapter 11 of the Letter to the Hebrews, tells the full tale of obedience.

It is on the basis of this deeply rooted relationship between obedience and faith, seen in the biblical perspective, that we can speak of "faith" in Christ. We can leave aside texts that speak of the "faith of Christ" where the implications of the use of the genitive are not clear, as well as the texts which suppose in Christ an absolute faith in the sense of confidence (cf. Mt 17,17–21). There remains the magnificent and conclusive statement in the Letter to the Hebrews (10,5–10) which brings us what we may call the "objective" of the Incarnation. And this text in turn finds its ultimate counterpart in the still more magnificent hymn in Philippians (2,5–11). These two texts are quite different in style but as regards their theological content they are inseparable. The Letter to the Hebrews takes the terminology of Psalm 40,7–9 as it was commonly understood in the Greek translation: "A body thou hast prepared for me". But the Masoretic text – the Hebrew one produced by the "men of tradition" dating from the sixth century A.D. – had "ears thou hast dug for me", meaning you have intensified my sense of hearing in readiness to pay attention and obey. This matches the text of the Third Song of the Servant of Yahweh in Isaiah 50,4–5: "Morning by morning he wakens, he wakens my ear to hear as those who are taught. The Lord God has opened my ear".

In his 1516–1517 commentary on the Letter to the Hebrews, Luther used the Hebrew version of Psalm 40 and declared that of all the senses hearing alone characterises the Christian. Obviously that is a formula which reflects the assessment and priority of faith which he already held. We can recognise the veracity and even the depth and beauty of that formula without making the point that Luther still belonged to the Catholic Church at that time. It is true that very real differences between Protestantism and Catholicism can be traced back to the diverse positions each came to give to the spoken word and presence (and, as occasion arose, in the context of sacrament). But if we take a sound thinker like Aquinas, with his touch of a Greek frame of thought and his habit of subjecting everything to an ontological analysis, surely we find that on this subject he yet again exhibits an objective and genuinely Christian grasp of things. It is perfectly true that with his Aristotelian philosophy he holds that sight is more spiritual and more reliable than hearing. But it is equally true that Aquinas declared that the religious outlook of Israel is governed by its characteristic reliance on *auditus*, hearing the word, whereas the Christian characteristically adds to that the gift of grace conferred by a sacrament, with special reference to Baptism and Eucharist. But Aquinas is also aware that sight can only have superiority if the object to be perceived is well and truly present and the person in question is here and now capable of absorbing what is being conveyed. On the other hand hearing takes priority when in order to acquire knowledge of something we need to learn about it from someone else. That is the case of things beyond our understanding. This is why hearing is so overwhelmingly important for us Christians in this life on earth. What distinguishes our situation here is our dependence on faith in what is communicated to us by the spoken word, whereas in the life to come we shall perceive by vision. Not surprisingly in the New Testament and in the Old, the verb "to see" is used in passages about the after-life (eschatology) and with reference to God it is put in the future tense. "Hearing" attributed to God corresponds to hearing by human beings. God calls to us and requires us to listen to what he says and we, in our turn, ask him to listen to us: "Lord, hear my voice. Let your ears be attentive to the voice of my pleading".

Hearing and seeing

We must not however make the mistake of thinking that, either with the Old Testament or still less with the New, we can give priority to "hearing" to the extent of completely excluding "seeing", as though it was quite out of place or even a positive distortion. The Word was made flesh, not a spoken sound. Protestant authors show a tendency to reduce everything systematically to the spoken word and to present visible manifestations in both Testaments as though they were just ratifications of the statements made by the spoken word. And they similarly treat the sacraments as nothing more than *verbum visibile*, "visible word". It is true that the sacramental signs, like the "signs" in the Gospel, depend on the spoken word for their signification. But to that the signs add their specific value: that is the meaning of the term *ex opere operato* as affirmed by the Council of Trent.

The theology of the Eastern Churches takes the opposite stand. It is alive with the idea of experiencing light and a desire to see. Oriental mysticism thinks of spiritual perfection as *theoria*, contemplation, and has thus developed a complete theology of God-revealing light. The Orthodox Church has devised a perfect self-portrait in the Feast of Orthodoxy which was instituted in 843. It celebrates the victory of the supporters of the cult of images over the iconoclasts. There is a marked connection between this and the Semitic milieu of Syria and the influence of the Anatolian soldiers. But the basis of the Orthodox attachment to icons is a profound theology of the Incarnation and the decisive transformation it brought about in the messianic regime with regard to visual representation.

In reflecting on all this we must not allow ourselves to become enmeshed in the kind of opposition some exegetes and historians have seen between biblical revelation achieved through "voice and ear" and the "inborn paganism of the Greek world" which seeks to reach God "by means of visual representation": as some would put it, the contrast between the "truly religious people who

28

hear God and are conscious of being in his presence" and the "aesthetes who are bent on perceiving visually". There is a kind of idolatry of the written and spoken word which is no less harmful than the idolatry of the graven image, and although biblical revelation is indeed a revelation of the spoken word, it is not only that. The theophanies of the Old Testament suggest that the spoken word is transcended by vision and that the whole Bible teems with a nostalgic yearning to see God. Indeed God uses the humanity of Christ as a means of manifesting his glory. If God was of his nature visible he would not be God and would not command our interest . . . The God of the New Testament is no less invisible than he is in the Old Testament. The new sign is to be found in the way the risen Christ disappears. He makes himself present. He shows himself to his chosen disciples so as to make them realise that he is the selfsame Christ they have known and that he is truly alive. And then he suddenly disappears, quite simply because now he is in his glory and is once more with the Father, the invisible God. What he leaves us is a human image of God, the "humanity of God"[1]

This distinctive principle of the New Testament has been an abundant source of spiritual aspiration and artistic inspiration throughout the history of Christianity. Christianity cannot be reduced to sheer submissiveness stripped of joy nor to a kerygma devoid of culture. There is something about the life of the Church which ensures that even in the frailty of our human existence here on earth it catches something of the radiant joy of those who already see God face to face in heaven. Dante's Paradiso (Canto XXVII) puts it impressively:

"Al Padre, al Figlio, allo Spirito Santo"
cominciò 'gloria' tutto il paradiso,
si che m'inebriava il dolce canto.
Ciò ch'io vedeva mi sembrava un riso
del universo; per che mia ebbrezza
intrava per l'udire e per lo viso.

1. H. de Lubac, *La Révélation Divine*. Traditions Chrétiennes (Cerf 1983).

"Glory to Father, Son and Holy Spirit",
Burst forth the whole of paradise,
Swept was I into ecstasy,
So sweet the heavenly song.
I saw what seemed a smiling universe,
And rapture flooded into me
through eyes and ears alike.

Chapter 3

A God who has spoken *

*"Thy words were found and I ate them; thy words
became to me a joy and the delight of my heart" (Jer 15,16).*

Our God is a God who speaks and addresses himself to us.
However amazing that may sound it is understandable
when we recall that he is a Person and we, too, created to
his image and likeness, are persons. God has spoken in the
past: "In many and various ways God spoke of old
through the prophets; but in these last days he has spoken
to us by a Son" (Heb 1,1–2).

In many and various ways! Many of them are unknown
to us. What form, for instance, did the word of God take
when he spoke to Adam, to the very first member of
humankind emerging from the animal kingdom some
three million years ago? Or what of the word of God to
Abraham 1800 years B.C.? The written account of it that
has come down to us was made a thousand years after the
event itself took place. It was rather like having the history
of the sons of Charlemagne written up for the first time
today . . . And then we can also ask whether God has
spoken to those millions of people who have lived without
contact with what we call *the* Revelation or who are in that
situation today. Has he spoken to the men who were
moved to start to nurture many religions that are unknown
to us?

We stand by our faith with certitude that God
intervened in the history of the human race — quite late
on when you think how old the human race is — with a
positive plan for an alliance with humankind and for its
salvation. We find this first in Genesis 12,1: "Now the
Lord said to Abram". A great, solemn and decisive point

---

* *Cahiers Saint-Dominique* (1978).

31

in history. What was initiated then still lives on in our lives today. A whole series of interventions has followed on, shaping our sacred history right down to Christ and his Apostles.

It has all been worked out and put down in writing by inspired men, though we do not always know their identity. And the writers were not taking down a dictated text as if their hand, as it held the pen clasped, was manipulated, so to speak, by Another. What happened was that deep down in themselves an urge to write came from God and God kept watch over their writing in such a way that we can, and indeed must, see it as attributable to him and linked with the fulfilment of his plan for alliance and salvation.

But besides these there are other writings belonging to Israel and bearing on Christ which, unlike those we have just been describing, are not inspired. There are about fifty such Jewish writings and about fifty Christian ones which are known under impressive names. To distinguish them from inspired writings we call them Apocrypha. To make the distinction clear, towards the middle of the second century a list (a canon) was drawn up of the Scriptures recognised by the Church as inspired, that is, the Word of God. These are known as the canonical books, the ones normative of the Church's beliefs and life. As regards the Old Testament the Church adopted the Jewish canon, if not the one used by the Jews of Palestine at any rate the one of the Jews who lived amongst the Greeks and were in some measure influenced by the way Greeks expressed themselves. Anyway, the Christian Church accepted the whole of the Old Testament. One of the first heresies the Church ever had to deal with was that of Marcion, around the middle of the second century. He rejected the Old Testament because, he said, it presented God as rigid and cruel. Although the second century was a time when the young Church found in Judaism a powerful adversary, it declared that it is not possible to come to Christ except by way of the patriarchs and prophets. And even today the body of our Divine Office (the Prayer of the Church) is made up of the Jewish psalms. As regards the Scriptures connected with Christ and Christianity the criterion by which they are listed as canonical is apostolic in origin. By that we do not mean that they came from the hands of one or another of the twelve Apostles. Only two of the four Gospels (Matthew and John) did and several of the letters may well have come from other hands. What we mean is that they date back to "apostolic times", that is to say, a brief period of essential shaping and inauguration and therefore definitively normative.

This notion of a normative criterion also applies to the faith and life of the People of God as such. And this supposes something characteristically "public", taking that term as the precise opposite of what concerns purely a private individual. Among God's communications with human beings there are some that are spoken interiorly to an individual, private revelations as they are called, and these do not belong to what God communicates to his people in order to constitute them as such and give them a structure resting on definitive foundations.

Ways of reading the Bible

So, then, there we have our Bible. And it is there to be read. But there are several ways of reading it. One is to see it purely and simply as history, and that approach can be either quite simplistic or scientific and critical. Anyone can indulge in the simplistic approach. But the scientific and critical reading supposes technical ability, knowledge of ancient languages, of archaeology and historical, geographical and cultural settings. Obviously it is only the experts who can carry out that sort of work, but all the same they can make us aware of their findings both in books and articles and in the introduction and notes to those excellent translations of the Bible which we have today. It all offers us a real feast of understanding.

But there is much more to it than even that. From the end of the eighteenth century and throughout the nineteenth, Protestants, especially Germans, and from the beginning of the twentieth century Catholics as well, have worked out finely adjusted methods of analysing and assessing biblical texts. Père Lagrange's studies of the historical method date back to 1903. They first worked on the Old Testament. There they brought to light evidence that the texts had sometimes been rewritten or re-compiled and a variety of sources and documents had been drawn on in the process. It transpired that Exodus was not actually written by Moses: it records his death, anyway. Different parts of the book of Isaiah had been written by different authors and at successive dates. This gave rise to all sorts of questions and difficulties. When Vatican II began, attention was being focussed on the Gospels, then on the Acts and then on the Pastoral Letters. The historical form and historical transmission theories showed that certain passages of the Gospel presented the faith of the early Christian community rather than the actual words uttered by Christ. But people were left wondering what to make of all this, all the more so because biblical scholars disagreed among themselves. What one had laboriously worked out another would come along and demolish, only to have his views challenged by yet another.

At Vatican II, both in the assembly and in the "corridors", many an ardent battle was fought. The bishops, on getting into their buses in St Peter's Square after a morning session, might find leaflets on their seats attacking especially the Roman Biblical Institute and accusing it of modernism. The attacks were launched mostly by lecturers at the Lateran. Pope Paul VI went there one day and told them pretty roundly to lay off. The Biblical Institute itself had a lucid and convincing champion in the person of Cardinal Bea who had once held the post of director there. Nevertheless at the beginning of the Council not a single member of the academic staff of the Institute nor from the Ecole Biblique de Jerusalem was appointed a *peritus*, that is a member of the body of expert consultants to the Council. That was remedied during the Council.

Three things were involved which were to provide the subject matter for the Dogmatic Constitution on Divine Revelation (*Dei Verbum*) which was eventually promulgated on 18 November 1965.

1. Firstly there was the question of the relation between Scripture and Tradition. An ardent debate took place on this in the Council assembly as early as 14 November 1962, just a month after the opening of the Council. During the debate members already began to take sides on the issue under discussion and at the same time most of them began to sense what the atmosphere of the Council was going to be like. The draft text presented to the Council by the preparatory commission, which had been at work before the Council began, envisaged Scripture and Tradition as two distinct sources of Revelation, which meant that there could be truths revealed by God by way of an oral tradition that were not revealed at all in Scripture. But that kind of statement will just not do, for there is not a single dogma held by the Church on scriptural grounds alone and not a single one held on the strength of oral tradition alone. Besides, Scripture and Tradition are not two separate sources of Revelation but two means that we have to combine in order to grasp fully the meaning of the Word of God. Hence after close and lively scrutiny, during which two quite different frames of mind confronted each other, the draft text was voted out on 20 November 1962. An article in the French Jesuit monthly, *Études*, labelled that date "the end of the Counter Reformation".

At this point the draft text — Pope John XXIII gave it the irenic title "Concerning Divine Revelation" — was handed over to be worked on first to a commission consisting of theologians and members of the Secretariat for Unity and then to a sub-committee of the Theological Commission. It was agreed from the start that any wording that might directly or by implication suggest the idea that Scripture and Tradition were two independent sources would be rigorously banned.

2. Secondly, ever since the rise of Scholasticism, Catholic theology, catechesis and preaching has been

nurtured by a markedly intellectualist notion of Revelation. Of course there can be no question of caricatures like "God speaking from the clouds" or "truths dropping down from heaven". The point we are making is that Revelation was seen as a communication of pronouncements which together make up a depository of truths and that it was up to the Magisterium to clarify and define them and that the job of theologians is to work away at that and draw conclusions which some day might also be susceptible of definition. As a matter of fact some of the members of the Preparatory Theological Commission, which was put to work before the Council, toyed with the idea that the Council would formulate new Marian doctrines (dogmas?) like the queenship of Mary, mediation, co-redemption.

As things turned out, *Dei Verbum* in a brief opening chapter made a firm statement which spelt out a broader and more biblical notion of Revelation and therefore of faith. It has, as the document shows, three distinctive traits:

a) The purpose of Revelation is alliance, that is to say, sharing, communion, with God. That implies relations with him as person to person and, though we would never have presumed to say it had not God himself said it first, as friend to friend.

b) Revelation is not realised only by use of spoken words but also by deeds, happenings, though these are indeed accompanied by words which bring to light what they are meant to convey. For instance, the exodus from Egypt, the death and resurrection of Christ, are in themselves events which convey Revelation. A parallel statement may be made concerning Tradition, namely that it is not purely oral but also a communication of realities, as for instance in the case of the sacraments.

c) Holding on to these two traits we discover that Christ is the fulness of Revelation, not only because of what he taught but also taken as the reality which he himself is and because of what he has done for us. Clearly that is of the utmost importance for our reading of the Scriptures, including the Old Testament. The whole of Scripture

36

converges on Christ and speaks of him. Christ is the sum total of what Scripture conveys.

3. Thirdly, hand in hand with the intellectualist notion of Revelation there went an equally intellectualist notion of faith. To make an act of faith meant essentially accepting certain truths on the absolute authority of God who conveyed them, and that authority was seen in some sort as shared by the Church (hierarchy) who handed the truths on to us. Accepting an authority implies obedience and the operative role of obedience can certainly not be erased from the definition of faith: the Scriptures make that clear. It is equally certain that faith is not just words we mouth: it has a substantial content and therefore a dogmatic aspect, as H. Duméry has clearly shown. But faith is a much richer reality than the idea of it that was customarily presented. *Dei Verbum* gives a closely-worded definition of it: "By faith man freely commits his entire self to God making the full submission of his intellect and will to God who reveals" (*DV* 5). The intellectual aspect of faith is brought out, even with a quotation from Vatican I to support it, but it is seen as integrated in an upsurge of self-commitment to God so that our lives may be directed by him.

How Dei Verbum *means us to read the Scriptures*

1. God has indeed spoken but he has used human language and our ways of communicating, our kind of narrative and phraseology, and not in a timeless language, for there is no such thing. So we find for instance in the part of the Bible about David the narrative and language is that of the tenth century B.C.; in Jeremiah that of the seventh and in Paul and John that of their time and setting. Thus each period has its own particular contemporary type of narrative and style in keeping with its culture, pattern of life and object. *Dei Verbum* fully recognises this historical setting of the Word of God, its "incarnation", its *kenosis*, expressed traditionally as God's condescension putting himself on a footing with

human beings. It is interesting to note that Pius XII had already led the way in this reading of Scripture in the perspective of awareness of historical setting. You can see it for instance in his Encyclical *Divino Afflante Spiritu* (30 September 1943) and his Letter to Cardinal Suhard (16 January 1948). However, as the attack we have referred to above on the Biblical Institute showed, something more was needed. *Dei Verbum* provides an outright reply to that attack, stating clearly that the use of scientific means together with a critically enlightened reading is a way of pinpointing what the author of a given scriptural passage − and God through him − intended to convey. It follows that the sound, honest, balanced and unpretentious use of biblical science is demanded by the object and sheer purpose of exegesis. This entails a grasp of the difference which historical setting, use of language and literary *genre* can make to accurate understanding of Scripture. Thus there are in the Bible strictly historical accounts, for instance the life of David, and there are others that are cast in poetic form and even some that are more or less imaginary stories or fables told to drive home some truth or practical lesson. Esther and Jonah are examples of this. Then again there are meditations full of wisdom and apocalyptic types of literature with their bewildering perspective and imagery. All this has to be taken into account in order to ensure a thorough reading of the inspired Bible. Nowadays we are well supplied with useful tools for that purpose. Indeed one might be justified in thinking there is a bit too much of an itch for the scientific with the danger that the human element might stifle the divine.

2. In this connection we need to read No. 12 para. 3 and No. 23 of *Dei Verbum* and abide by what they say. They take us right into the heart of the Christian and Catholic approach to the Sacred Scripture. We are bidden bear in mind that they form a unit. True enough, different parts were written at different times in the course of a thousand years and they are stamped with the various circumstances and historical settings in which they were composed. But for all that a unity runs through them all, namely, the one

and only divine plan and pattern of salvation which ultimately has its centre, its fulfilment and its very meaning in the mystery of Christ. This ties up with what we said earlier on about the nature and the object of Revelation. A biblical scholar, in a study he made of how the canon of the Scriptures was drawn up, pointed out that the four Gospels listed in the canon each had peculiarities of its own and, if you get down to details, some real divergences. But the compilers of the canon were convinced that this in no way undermined their essential unity which is nothing short of a reflection of the unity of God himself and of his plan for alliance with humankind.

As we have already said, the Church respects their labours as they work away to discover a Paulinism, a Johanninism, a Lucan interpretation and so on. But we are not letting ourselves in for a divided faith echoing the Corinthians who split up, some saying they followed Peter, others Apollo, others Paul. It is to Tradition that we turn, especially to the Fathers of the Church and the Liturgy, for a synthesis of what is brought to us scattered through the pages of the Scriptures. That kind of synthesis will inevitably leave aside some divergences which could be lawfully and indeed profitably taken into account. But by focussing everything onto the very core of the Christian mystery — the Fathers do so by their commentaries and the Liturgy does it by its sheer act of worship — it brings out the unity that knits together this very considerable diversity. It is from that synthesis that we, in union with the Church, can learn the proper way to understand the Scriptures. *Dei Verbum* takes up the traditional theme of the twofold repast in which we receive the Bread of Life, which is Christ: in it we are fed with both the Word and the Eucharist. The Mass gives us this perfect bread. If we make the Fathers and the Liturgy, that is the Church, our home and dwell in it, the nagging problem of divergences between the Christ of history and the Christ of faith is soothed away. Quite simply, they merge with each other.

What we have as a result is "spiritual reading". That does not mean something nebulous, aesthetic or fanciful, but a reading done under the Holy Spirit. St Paul and St

John tell us that the meaning of the Scriptures, identical with the Christian mystery, is disclosed when we seek Christ in them with the help of the Holy Spirit (cf. 1 Cor 12,3; 2 Cor 3,13–18; 1 Jn 4,2). If Christ manifests and interprets the Father, so does the Holy Spirit interpret Christ for us. We must therefore beg the help of the Holy Spirit. Indeed reading the Scriptures, like any other Christian act, calls for an invocation of the Holy Spirit. As a result the Word enshrined in the dead letter becomes a spiritual experience and a communication of life. We have the liberty and the joy which are the fruits of the Spirit. No wonder the study of the Scriptures used to be known as *lectio divina*, a Godward spell of reading.

3. No. 19 of *Dei Verbum* takes a firm stand on the historicity of the Gospels. It is a compact and balanced statement and demands unhurried reading. It points out that the glorious events of Christ – Easter, Pentecost . . . – and Christian experience enable the Apostles a "fuller understanding" of what Christ had said and done. This "supplement" to the bare narrative of events and repetition of utterances is traceable to the role of the Holy Spirit and the nature of witness. And thus it is that the Christ of history is comprised in the Christ of faith. Furthermore the paragraph of *Dei Verbum* in question points out that the Gospels are distinctive compositions and each of their writers had a particular objective in view, selecting particular episodes and phrases, focussing what they had in mind on a particular happening with which they were acquainted, shaping their narrative to the lesson they were out to convey. But in proceeding in this way the Evangelists' purpose (to quote *Dei Verbum*) "was that we might know the 'truth' concerning the things of which we have been informed" (cf. Lk 1,2–4).

4. Chapter Six of *Dei Verbum* deals with the place of the Scriptures in the life of the Church. Evidently the object is to encourage the diffusion of the Scriptures. The document makes the point that they must be the very life of theology and of preaching, that is to say not only homilies but religious education and pastoral instruction, including that given by the Magisterium. If we look around

40

we will realise that, thanks be to God, we are living in one of the most Bible-orientated ages ever. There are the liturgical readings, the frequent private use of the Bible, its place in preaching and in studies and the many publications about Scripture. And then there is what has been nicknamed the "Fifth Gospel", namely, pilgrimages to the Holy Land which throw fresh light on the meaning of the Bible texts for pilgrims. There are, however, some unfortunate gaps. There are so many people who have a Bible and would not be without one but hardly ever open it, let alone make use of it as daily nourishment from the Word of God. We may well ask ourselves how we stand in this respect.

Some people may find it rather a pity that the pronouncements and documents coming from our pastors so often owe more to impressive human wisdom than to the Word of God, whereas the latter would after all lend them unassailable value and command a better audience. Is *Dei Verbum* being over-optimistic when it says: "the Magisterium is not superior to the Word of God, but is its servant. It teaches only what has been handed on to it. At the divine command and with the help of the Holy Spirit, it listens to this devotedly, guards it with dedication and expounds it faithfully" (no. 10)?

Conclusions

The spirit of *Dei Verbum* tallies with the overall spirit of the Council. We might identify it with two characteristic traits which go hand in hand with each other:

a) It takes up the age-old Tradition and uses it as a means of coming to grips with the problem of the twentieth century. That Tradition stood for holding the different parts of Scripture together as a single whole, since the selfsame spirit throughout seeks to unfold the one and only mystery of the alliance with Christ. Origen and others carried typology so far that they ended up with subtle and questionable allegories. But basically what they were doing was presenting a "spiritual meaning" of the

Scriptures by focussing on their central fact. Thus this way of reading the Scriptures meant "seeing and believing", recognising the Son of God in Christ's human life in this world and listening to God himself speaking to us in the texts construed within particular cultural and historical settings.

b) "Holding together" is characteristic of *Dei Verbum*. Indeed that is true of the whole of Vatican II where papacy calls for collegiality and collegiality for papacy, "word" summons up "sacrament" and "sacrament" "word", the "people" envisages "pastor", "pastor" the "people", the celebrating Church is linked with the serving Church and the Church of the world with the Church for God, and Scripture goes with Tradition and Tradition with Scripture. It all brings us face to face with the theme we are pursuing here. No. 10 of *Dei Verbum* in particular stresses that Tradition, Scripture and Church (Magisterium) are "so connected and associated that one of them cannot stand without the others".

Chapter 4

Human response to call*

Animals have a built-in capacity for responding when they are called, in the sense that they react to incitement which may be caused, for domestic animals, by sundry sounds or by the sound of the human voice, and for other animals there is reponse to others of their own species, to danger and to prey. But for human beings response entails something altogether different.

Of course the human being is an animal and produces animal noises expressing pain and so on which alert others but also has the power of speech and there is nothing animal about that. Speech conveys thought and purpose. Addressed to others it is an invitation from person to person eliciting shared activity or companionship. Its most characteristic trait in terms of relations between persons is that it is an act of one free agent eliciting response from another free agent. If you know German you will recognise how this is illustrated by the association of *Wort* (word) and *Antwort* (answer).

Since God is a personal being and since he has made us to his image and likeness, it is quite natural that he should speak to us and that this should first of all take the form of a call to us. Of course he is not bound to do so, but once by his benevolence he has done so, we realise how fitting it is. What we can work out, once philosophy gets going on the topic, is that human beings have an in-built capacity to being called by God and to becoming aware of the special plan God freely designs for them, an awareness in which God reveals himself to humankind. One could illustrate this from the work of contemporary intellectuals such as

La Vie Spirituelle (April 1969).

Maurice Blondel and Karl Rahner. But that would be too technical for our present purpose.

This capacity for being called by God is for us human beings the sign of our transcendence and of endowment with free will. It shows that human beings are not moulded to a single inflexible stance nor limited to their inherent resources: that is precisely the mark of that transcendence. But this very transcendence places the person in a situation of free dependence towards other persons wishing to draw the other or bring the other to share in their activity. That is why Christianity, and we ought here to say Judaeo-Christianity since what we are pointing out is clearly found in the Old Testament, has always affirmed in human beings the combined personal freedom and dependence, autonomy and heteronomy, if we speak of heteronomy as used when the "other person" is closer to me than I am to myself and loves me more than I love myself since it is thanks to the "other person" that I possess the love I bear myself. That is why in Judaeo-Christianity the recognition that the human being is a free agent is always positively linked with the idea of the human being set in an environment native to the human being consisting of a hierarchical framework of beings which owe their origin and continuing existence to their creator.

That is exactly what Thomas Aquinas teaches. Recent studies of him show more clearly than ever the penetrating grasp he had of the human person as a free and productive agent. But he is equally emphatic in applying to the human person in regard to the supernatural vocation, be it noted, a totally general principle of a cosmological or, more precisely, a cosmic kind. We find this in a tract in which Aquinas investigates whether it is necessary for salvation to believe things which are beyond the natural powers of the intellect to grasp. There are realities which are not totally self-contained entities but are inserted in a much more extensive entity and are thus part of a structured order of things. Such realities can derive their perfection from two sources: from themselves, that is from their own resources and their in-built stimulus; from something of a higher order than themselves and a stimulus communicated to them by that superior reality. There are things we can get to know by our own unaided powers and there is knowledge to which we can be lifted up if a mind superior to ours makes its thoughts known to us. That is exactly what happens through Revelation. God calls us to himself and speaks to us and we respond to his invitation by faith.

Christian life is founded entirely on the possible occurrence of this call or, more accurately, on the reality of such a call. Over and above the initial and fundamental call of faith there are other calls of an everyday kind, calls to serve others, in a word, to things quite ordinary and yet quite other than mere habit since each instance comes as a new and unforeseen call on our free response. A saint, it has been said, is someone always at the ready waiting for orders (Emilio Castro). And you do not change the subject when God is speaking to you! (Madeleine Delbrêl).

The most striking instance of the effect of this capacity for hearing and responding is conversion. A human being is open to changing, to seeing life and its meaning in a perspective which to the individual in question is quite new. That is exactly what is implied in the admonition of Jesus and of John the Baptist echoed in the opening passages of the Gospel: "Repent, for the kingdom of heaven is at hand"[1]. Surely that is why Jesus takes as his starting point the situation of the sinner. He is always out to fill a crying need. It is to the deprived that he wants to bring enrichment. And indeed deep down it is only those who are impoverished who can be enriched, for as he has said: "Those who are well have no need of a physician, but those who are sick" (Mt 9,12).

Luther, quoting this text in 1515–1516, aligned it with Luke 15,4 and said that it is only the lost sheep that is sought, the captive liberated, the poor enriched, the infirm made whole, only a void is filled and the humbled exalted and a structure built where there was nothing before.

St Ambrose, who was instrumental in the conversion of St Augustine, grasped the special place thus assigned to the sinner and made it his model. Reflecting on the passage

---

1. John the Baptist: Mk 1,4; Mt 3,2ff. For Jesus: Mk 1,15; Mt 4,17.

in Genesis where God calls Adam after his fall, hiding himself from sight out of his sense of guilt, Ambrose says: "The Lord called the man and said: 'Where are you?' The just man who sees the Lord and dwells with him does not hide himself from his presence nor does he have to be called to come to him, for he is with the Lord already. But the sinner who has made himself deliberately deaf to the voice of the Lord and hides himself amongst the bushes of Paradise is the one God calls to, saying, 'Adam, where are you?' He is hiding, covered with shame. But the sheer fact that God calls to him is a sign that he can be cured of his sin, for God calls those on whom he has pity".

We of course are not going to imitate children who do something naughty because they know full well that they will be petted and cuddled after they have been scolded. What we need to do is simply to be vividly aware of our condition as sinful people and of the need in which we stand of constant daily conversion and drilling ourselves so that every aspect of our being and our life comes under the influence of the Gospel. "Repent", in the Gospel meaning of the word, is part and parcel of all Christian life at every instant.

Having established the existence of this capacity to respond to a call and its significance in terms of the human being's joint transcendence and dependence, we may ask ourselves what kind of obstacles might impede its effective operation.

First of all, obviously, there are types of philosophy that radically reject that transcendence and dependence. It has rightly been said — in keeping with Hosea 11,1 — that the typical human person envisaged in the Bible is one whom God is teaching to walk. But there are those who want to go along on their own and will not stand for letting others teach them how to walk. That is the case of the philosophers who uphold the absolute autonomy of individual free choice. The well-known French author Sartre makes a character in one of his books, *Les Mouches*, say: "Heaven has nothing to offer, neither good or ill nor anyone to give me orders, for I, O Jupiter, am a human being and each human being has to create his own way of life for

46

himself''. Jean Lacroix has said that what Sartre is really doing here is to work out what he means by man's vocation. For him, being free means constantly renewing and reshaping oneself, deciding for oneself what one's existence shall be, not being fixedly pledged to anything.

Albert Camus is in much the same position. He gave as one of his reasons for being an atheist that to admit the existence of God would be to deny one's right to choose for oneself the way one wants to lead one's life and so impair one's freedom.

One does not have to jettison genuine human freedom and responsibility in order to refute these philosophies but what one has to ask is how a philosophy which is nothing more than an existential anthropology can possibly take on board the notion of vocation and, therefore, that characteristic transcendence whereby the human being is open to a renewal from above in terms of a call. Man/woman must be seen as belonging to a universe which he/she has not devised even though he/she is able to assess it and modify it. The human person's creativity is confined to a set framework and predetermined limits. And that does not reduce the person to the level of a mere thing or the sheer realities of the natural order. All it is doing is quite simply to recognise the facts of human condition, namely that it does not bring about its own structure and setting but is essentially pre-structured and pre-situated.

The more discoveries scientific research makes the more aware we become of the multitude of beings and forces that envelope us to an extent we would never have realised when scientific knowldge was still quite elementary. The world is full of all kinds of radiation though our powers of perception severely restrict our awareness of them. We have only to stop and think what it means to us to be able to perceive light and colour and the outward shape of things. And just imagine how much we would miss if we had no eyes to see with. Many of our fellow human beings are indeed deprived of sight and a whole universe that surrounds them consequently does not exist for them. But there are many other radiations that none of us perceive.

It even happens that some animals are better endowed than we are in one way or another. They can see infra-red light and hear ultra-high sounds that our eyes and ears do not register. Bats — so it is said — have a sort of radar thanks to which they avoid bumping into things in the dark. We make good our natural deficiences by the use of instruments which we have invented.

But however short we may fall of some animals in one or another way, we excel them all beyond measure by our ability to register a vocal communication — a call — from another person. The air around us which serves as a medium to carry the sound of the bark of a dog is also the medium of the spoken word by which one mind communicates with another, transmitting its thoughts, its call, its love. Some individuals are better endowed than others in this ability to register communications of this kind coming from another. There is something of a touch of the prophetic and priestly about it, a precious gift, for even without realising it people emit signals of distress, calls for help, offered love and invitations to collaborate. God himself does this uniquely in his divine way: "My son, give me your heart" (Prov 23,26). The original text might well be rendered, "My son, my daughter, focus your attention on me". The fact is that the word for "heart" in Hebrew means everything within a human being that produces thoughts and sentiments and determines our habitual frame of mind. And one fundamental factor in that is concentration of attention. This is a quality which biblical tradition and, in its wake, Jewish tradition, have bequeathed to Christians. We may be tempted to imagine that this tradition has fallen into disuse. Père Louis Bouyer has shown that this is far from true and has spelt out a clear lesson for us on the subject in the following terms: in Judaism, more than in almost any other religion, the great masters of spirituality have striven constantly to safeguard against the mechanical recital of prayers which drains them of their true content. This is one of the most constant themes of rabbinical teaching. It insists that prescribed prayers are denuded of all value and do not deserve to be called prayers at all unless they are accompanied with what it calls *kawannah*. The rabbinical Hebrew term is of the same root as a verb meaning to concentrate attention. It conveys the kind of interior dispositions of persons whose mind and heart are kept constantly alert to the sacred realities to which the wording of vocal prayers reach out, and alertness fostered by the spirit of faith with which they say their prayers and their total absorption in the meaning of the words they pronounce[2].

This leads to say a word about obstacles that impede response to the kind of call we have been dealing with, quite apart from the brand of existentialism which simply dismisses any notion of autonomy rooted in personal freedom. Today we are subjected to a hundred and one distractions that leave us dazed and shatter our chances of registering ideas and quiet reflection. There is noise and turbulence and tenseness, music with no rhyme or reason to it, songs clean out of touch with reality, an incessant stream of pictures that flash past before you can take them in. We are bombarded with publicity, journalistic sensationalism and "exclusive" stories, more often than not blatant scandal, and no end of instances of people kicking over the traces and made to look as though they are the "in" thing.

There is no escaping from that world around us unless we were to set up isolated little islands of peace and quiet. But what we can and must do is to maintain deep down within ourselves the effective means of listening to God and readiness to welcome him when he calls on us. There is an imprescriptible truth which, for example, is borne out in Père Alphonse Gantry's books *Les Sources* and *Souvenir de ma jeunesse*. He himself rediscovered the Augustinian theme of interior self-control and took it as a practical guide. You do not have to adopt a platonistic system of thought and of the human being in order to appreciate the truth of this theme. Everyone with alert awareness of the spiritual life has experienced it. And like all experience it can only be

2. Louis Bouyer, *Eucharistie* (DDB 1966).

realised if certain conditions are fulfilled, the first of which in this case is readiness to cut down on frivolous curiosity and dissipation. Call it asceticism or mortification or just a healthy principle, if you will, but one just cannot succeed without it. Of course God can make himself heard however loud the din, and closed doors do not prevent Christ from coming in if he so wishes. All the same, the ordinary and surest way of not failing to hear is quite simply to listen. In the words of Psalm 45: "Hear, O daughter, consider and incline your ear"[3].

3. See Chapter 2, *Listening and Seeing*, above.

Chapter 5

The mystery of encounter

We had better define our terms. "Encounter" is a quite straightforward word but here it is going to entail not only people but circumstances and events as well, in a word, everything that happens as we go our way. As to the word "mystery", it is true that it is often misused. But it is the right word to use here in its two-fold aspect as a religious term. First, it is used to denote the mysterious, in other words anything that is beyond our grasp. Secondly, as we find it in the terminology of the Fathers and in theological usage, it denotes a deep reality having a meaning and an effect beyond what we are capable of spontaneously perceiving. The adjective that goes with the noun "mystery" is "mystical". In this sense, prior to the eleventh century the Eucharist was called the "mystical Body". To all intents and purposes the words "mystery" and "sacrament" were interchangeable. Hence at that period the word "sacrament" was used when speaking of the consecration of a church, or religious profession, the death of the faithful and so on. The key to this dynamic sacramental usage of the word "mystery" is the connection between the things to which it is applied and the divine plan which unfolds in the course of our human history and will find its ultimate fulfilment and significance in the eschatology. The plan itself can be designated by various terms descriptive of its content. Thus it is called the salvation of the world, the object of the *agape* of God or of his "philanthropy", to pick out a term from the Letter to Titus. In so far as that *agape* and "philanthropy" have been brought to us in Jesus Christ, they are identified with the Servant of the prophecies.

51

And, as we know, all this has its sequel in the Church which is the People of God and the Body of Christ, the universal sacrament of salvation and thus servant, sign and instrument of the *agape* and of the "philanthropy" of God. That is why the reflections we are about to make in talking about our personal existence can be applied to the Church and have an ecclesiological significance. For it is not only the institutions and objective means of grace that constitute the ecclesial sacrament of salvation: it applies equally to the People of God as such.

Encounter with persons

When you encounter another person you never really know exactly whom you are meeting. You think you do know the person but in fact you only have a very superficial knowledge. The worst mistake you can make is to stick a ready-made label on to people, slotting them into stock-in-trade category: communist, well-to-do, Samaritan, whatever. . . The Scriptures have plenty of instances that put us wise on this matter.

Abraham saw three men coming in the heat of the day (cf. Gen 18). He welcomed them and showed himself the perfect host. You remember the sequel. The question was who exactly they were. Angels perhaps? That is what the Letter to the Hebrews suggests. But, as you read on, it all seems to add up to a visit from God. In our Christian typology it is expressed as *"tres vidit et unum adoravit"*, he saw three yet one only did he adore, three people, but one God. Now take the case of Christ staggering under the weight of the cross. The Roman soldiers commandeer a man called Simon of Cyrene, who was making his way home from the fields, and make him carry the cross (cf. Mk 15,21). Simon was tired out, he wanted to get home and start preparing for tomorrow's Paschal feast. He may well have shown his resentment. He did not know whose cross it was he was really carrying nor what that particular cross would prove to be in the history of the world. The Gospel describes him as the father of Alexander and Rufus, two people evidently well known to the Christian community to whom the Gospel was addressed. It all suggests that Simon came to know what that cross meant and became a Christian along with his family.

In the case of Simon and the carrying of the cross Christ was physically present. But we know that ever since the Son of God assumed our human nature we must recognise a presence of Christ in every Christian and indeed in every one of our human beings. If Christ did not actually say: "You have seen your brother and have seen your Saviour", that statement does nevertheless convey an affirmation that runs throughout the Gospels, namely, that in every disciple, even the lowliest − in fact more especially the lowliest − we encounter Christ. You have only to read Mark 9,41, Mark 10,40–42, Matthew 18,5 and Luke 9,48. And Luke 10,16 and John 13,20 show that this is also true of Christ's envoys. It is open to question whether the narrative about the Judgement in Matthew 25 envisages in this way only the Christian brethren or in general all who are insignificant, poor, needy and down-trodden. The present writer opts for the latter interpretation. It seems to have a firm basis in Christology. The sheer fact of the Incarnation gives to every human encounter a theological and Christological dimension.

Even in the purely natural order human beings make an impact on one another and exercise an influence on one another's condition. And so does the world around us. Everything affects our senses. From the spiritual point of view an encounter between persons is not merely something neutral. It can be an opportunity for both parties to give and receive from each other something of spiritual worth such as St Paul expected from his encounter with the Christians at Rome (cf. Rom 1,11–12). Just what these passing encounters contribute to our ultimate destiny and that of those we meet we shall never know in this life. We each receive according to our particular capacity, which is part of that mysterious make-up of each one of us and which is known to God but which we ourselves can scarcely put our finger on. We have precious little knowledge of the impact we make on others, nor need we be all that much aware of the sort of impact we ought to make, such as how we should love them and help them in precisely their particular mysterious make-up and their particular development.

All this clearly calls for a type of spirituality and pastoral ministry characterised by openness to others with sensitivity and alertness to opportunities and encounters that present themselves. Who knows who it may be that God means us to meet. And who can tell just where we fit into his plan for salvation. St Paul says that all "Christians are created in Christ for good works which God has prepared beforehand, that we should walk in them" (Eph 2,10). This applies especially to every priest. For a priest is a sign for all to see of God's philanthropy. And furthermore his vocation is to reveal Jesus Christ and bring people into contact with him, and he is given the grace for that task and is equipped to play that role in the destiny of those whom he encounters. When you get down to the details and the precise individuals involved, the divine plan for salvation seems to be realised in circumstances that have all the appearance of being pure chance. One could quote dozens of instances from the Bible. Take Acts 8,26 where Philip is sent off down an utterly deserted road and there meets up with someone and ends up baptising him. Or there is the case, in Acts 9,10, of Ananias who was singled out and made ready for his encounter with Saul. The encounters are as freely given as grace. Yet sensitivity to a given occasion can vary considerably. Blessed indeed are those who, engaged as they are in their ordinary everyday run of life, are always alert to detect the unexpected and unusual happening. We might quote in this respect the elderly Simeon. The rite of purification of young mothers was a commonplace event for him. But thanks to the Spirit who dwelt in him and stimulated by that Spirit he was able to recognise the messianic happening in what looked like just another legal purification (cf. Lk 2,25).

For the Spirit is in fact the one who constantly prepares the way for the Gospel in advance, in prevision of events yet to come. He is the means by which the "mystery" of

54

Christ is unfolded progressively towards the ultimate goal of eschatology. He opens the door and makes people realise that it has been opened for God's purpose, as St Paul puts it in one of his favourite expressions (cf. 1 Cor 16,8–9; 2 Cor 2,12; Col 4,3; Acts 14,27).

The disposition for this openness to others is an eminently apostolic and pastoral quality. The author of the Pastoral Letters says that the Servant of the Lord must be "kindly to everyone" (2 Tim 2,24). This trait became so important and specific in ecclesiastical Tradition that it was seen as something much more than a readiness to give a warm welcome to others. This is illustrated by the episode that took place on the evening of Easter day on the road to Emmaus, so well brought out by St Gregory in his remarkable homily: "The Lord joined the two disciples without letting them know who he was. He tested them. Since they could not yet love him as God, perhaps at least they could love him as a pilgrim". When, in 1204, Innocent III approved the opening of the hospice of the Order of the Holy Spirit in Rome, he defined hospitality as the compendium of all the good works listed in Matthew 25,31–46. It is a welcome extended not only with affection but also with efficiency to everyone we are able to help.

Encountering happenings

What we have said about encounter with persons applies likewise to how we meet the routine happenings of everyday life as well as other events that arise. Just as we cannot really know what sort of person it is we meet, as we have said, nor precisely what kind of impact we are expected to make on them and receive from them, so also the exact manner of our involvement in events is something we cannot foresee. There is no end of illustrations of this in the Bible, since it is of the very essence of sacred history. A good instance is the attitude of David after the prophecy of Nathan. It is spelt out in David's prayer of thanksgiving (cf. 2 Sam 7,18–29). David is conscious that God has committed him to something quite beyond him, namely, the building of a "house" at some undetermined time in the future and with no foreseen limits. But when eventually we come to read the prayer spoken by Solomon at the dedication of that "house" (the Temple) we perceive that although the occasion is certainly one of genuine religious splendour, the atmosphere of challenged incapacity and incomprehension stretching into the unknown has vanished. The original promise has been fulfilled by the fact that Solomon has built the Temple. The ethos of prophecy is absent in the reign of Solomon. Its place has been taken by a "wisdom" which interprets the form things take there and then and the enigmas that currently present themselves.

The mystery of human options

The present is constantly and unconsciously geared to the future and the options we make at the present moment have consequences far beyond what we have in mind when we make them. We know this from our own experience and the Bible bears witness to it from cover to cover. The Old Testament, as J. Guillet said, presents a wide range of choices in which human beings are involved. On the face of it this commitment to options is not an exclusively biblical thing. The fable about Hercules at the crossroads having to choose between virtue and vice is an image of a commonplace experience. All the same there is something distinctive about the act of choosing portrayed in the Bible. The choice to be made is not between virtue and vice or between two options apparently diverse but in fact of equal value. The person choosing is always left considerably in the dark and the necessity of choosing is imposed by an authority that is somehow exclusive. No justification is offered for the demands made. It involves setting out on a path without knowing where it will ultimately lead and this will only be clarified bit by bit as one goes along.

We can discern three degrees of urgency in what we might call the measure of the mystery inseparable from our decision-making. Even at the purely human level of

Love and the plan of salvation

How, we may ask, do these notions apply to the problem of the salvation of people who have not yet been evangelised? The question may be expressed this way. Encounters with "God-the-unknown" may be the occasion for the germ of faith to be implanted and grow without the person involved being conscious of it. We should see this case above all in terms of the attitude we take towards another as a *person*. For a person is an absolute entity (some, like Maine de Biran, would say that the only notion of absolute reality we can conceive is the notion of person) and the only adequate relationship we can have with such a reality is a relationship of love. At this point the second order of things we have reflected on, namely, the encounter with events and the necessity of taking options, ties up with the first, the encounter with persons. We never know completely, as we have said, the implications of an action which we take nor what the outcome of our choice will be. Neither do we ourselves really know *who* it is we encounter. But on his side God is not some kind of sphinx playfully enmeshing humankind in enigmas nor an evil-minded supervisor only intent on catching his underlings out. God, who knows the misery hidden within each person as well as everything that happens and all the encounters that occur, marks out exactly where we fit into it all with a view to showing us his mercy and his love. His plan is a plan of salvation. He it is who truly loves all humankind.

Chapter 6

The Spirit in action*

This chapter is about the Holy Spirit, especially in regard to ecclesiology. The Pentecostal Movement will come into it because it has bearing on ecclesiology, though indeed in a wider context.

During Vatican II the Orthodox and Protestant observers were critical of the absence of pneumatology in the draft documents of the Council. This cropped up in a conversation with two Orthodox observers in particular. It was while the debate on *Lumen Gentium* was on. They said that if they had to draw up a draft document on the Church two chapters would be ample, one on the Holy Spirit and one on what living as a Christian means. Their criticism would have been sound enough if it had been levelled at one or another Catholic treatise which dealt with hardly anything but the theme of Hierarchy and failed to go into the transcendent principle of life and the life it engenders. One could quote in this connection the commentary on the 1877 Council by the well-known Jesuit, Dominic Palmieri. There is no mention of the Holy Spirit and only once is there reference to the text: "Where two or three are gathered together in my name there I am in the midst of them". A theologian of repute but decidely pre-conciliar in outlook remarked to one of the *periti* (specialist advisers) during Vatican II: "I see you speak about the Holy Spirit. Actually you know, it's the Protestants who do that. We Catholics have the Magisterium". We shall have more to say on that perspective later.

* *Proche-Orient Chrétien* (1973).

The Council really did work hard to satisfy the current demand for pneumatology. Unfortunately there is a notable lack of worthwhile studies of the Council from this angle, although there are reliable digests that are both interesting and stimulating. Anyway, as one observer remarked, the mere fact the Holy Spirit is being frequently mentioned (seventy times, actually, in *Gaudium et Spes*) will not of itself produce pneumatology. A Protestant theologian, G. Westphal, took it on himself to say that all the effort put into the Council document just ended up with topping the text off with the words "Holy Spirit" here and there. That assessment is quite unfair as it would be easy to prove. But it does stimulate us to look into the matter seriously and in the first place to ask ourselves what we understand by pneumatology.

Another Orthodox observer, Nikos Nissiotis, who was the most vocal in launching such attacks, has given the following description, rather than definition, of pneumatology. "Genuine pneumatology describes life and comments on it in the liberty of the Spirit and in the tangible communion of the historical Church whose essence is not found in itself nor in its institutions". That is not a very clear statement and undoubtedly the Orthodox would say that you cannot make one. We might offer this definition: Life in the freedom of the Spirit is the life of a Christian person as such, with his personal creativity. It is a life which the "establishment" (the Church in its structures) does not claim to determine exhaustively. It is a life that provides the basis for communion and calls for it. And by that is meant not just a vague communion of saints, an invisible Church, but the tangible communion of the Church. But, it must be borne in mind, it is inseparably linked with the grace which is bestowed on it from above. It does not possess within itself and as such its principle of sanctity and has to beg for it and receive it.

A good way of grasping what the current renewal of pneumatology stands for is to recall how things were presented in the past in the field of theology or at least in familiar patterns of thought. There can be no doubt that the Holy Spirit has never ceased to be active in the Church in innumerable ways and at all levels. And, indeed, the action of the Holy Spirit has always been present in the various areas of dogmatics. All the same there was something missing in the past.

First of all, take the theology of the Holy Trinity and the Third Person. There are good grounds for accepting that the Latin West is in no way inferior to the Syriac and Greek Eastern Churches in this respect. However, theology was inclined to follow the general trend of concentrating on issues which had been the focal points of polemics or of heresy. You can trace this, for instance, in the article on the Holy Spirit in the *Dictionnaire de Théologie Catholique* published in 1913. Articles in more recently published Dictionaries seem to be less preoccupied with such matters. And especially there has been an output of studies which either bring out all the wealth of Tradition or endeavour to reconstruct a theology of the Holy Spirit in God and in the economy of salvation, and sees both these aspects as inseparable from one another. There is, for instance, Heribert Mühlen with his insistence on the statement that if the Father is "I" and the divine Word is "Thou", the Spirit is "We in person", and presents the Church not as linked with the Incarnation, of which it is an extension (a notion inherited from Möhler by the 19th century Roman school) but with the outpouring of the Holy Spirit on Christ at the moment of his baptism. That is to say the selfsame Spirit, "We in Person", is in Christ and in the Church which is his Body.

There was in the past little mention of the Holy Spirit in sacramental theology except in speaking of his gifts in connection with the sacrament of Confirmation, a sacrament that was rather awkwardly handled by theologians and which somehow did not come alive, possibly precisely because of the lack of awareness of the mission of the Holy Spirit other than in the perspective of the mission of the divine Word. The absence of an *epiclesis* in the Mass of the Roman Rite is undoubtedly one reason why there has been little awareness in the West of the role of the Holy Spirit in the Eucharist — at the consecration

of the Species and in the reception of Holy Communion –
and this despite the many pointers to it in Western
theological writings, spiritual treatises and the lives of the
saints. The fact is that these pronouncements have borne
little fruit until recent years. The theological outlook has
greatly improved today.

True enough the Holy Spirit was evoked in ecclesiology,
but we need to see what form it took. The theme of the
Holy Spirit as the soul of the Church was derived from St
Augustine and was used as a basis for the rectitude of the
acts of the ecclesiastical institution. That largely explains
the reticence of Protestants in this context. In St
Augustine's teaching, the Holy Spirit, *caritas* and *unitas*
(charity and unity), intervenes out and above the
Christological institution of the Church's ministers and
the sacraments to produce salutary efficacity in the unity
of the *caritas* with which the entire *ecclesia*, that is to say,
the community of love, is endowed. In post-Scholastic
ecclesiology the Holy Spirit is seen as assuring the value
ex sese of the acts of the ecclesial institution, the sacraments and the dogmatic pronouncements. This was often
referred to at the time of the Council of Trent and at
the Council itself as a guarantee of fidelity to Tradition.
In modern times it has been evoked as a guarantee
of the pronouncements of the Magisterium. The
spiritual/personal aspects of the action of the Holy Spirit
were studied in spirituality and in an atmosphere
suggestive of what one might call today "privatisation".
In this connection there was also some deep and quite
extensive thinking about the indwelling of the Holy Spirit
on the pattern of Aquinas' presentation of them. But that
had little bearing on ecclesiology because the current
concept of man as a Christian was the outcome of a type
of anthropology derived precisely from an ecclesiology in
which the juridical factor in the Church as institution was
sometimes over-stated. Even charisms were seen as an
element in an individual's personal vocation and not as
something contributed to the organism of the living
Church. Charisms were referred to mostly in connection
with saints, for instance, holy founders of religious orders

and so on. And it was stated that in that way God had made proper provision at all times for the needs of the Church. That pretty well amounted once more to justifying the institutional concept.

We must be on our guard against painting too dismal a picture. The way we have presented the above description is something of an over-simplification. But it is not a caricature for all that. We must reaffirm quite clearly that the Holy Spirit was fully present in the life of the Church. We are simply saying that when it comes to examining the prevalent patterns of thought we discover an absence of pneumatological ecclesiology.

We note also that a change has been taking place. We may now examine what has provoked it and the main lines it has followed.

It would seem to have been sparked off by the growing place occupied by the laity in the Church. Formerly, when the image of "Church" was that of a powerful body — "an army arrayed for battle", to quote a favourite expression of the time — the clergy dominated the scene and ran the Church. Pretty well the only role left to the laity was to defend the Church in the field of public life and politics. Within the confines of the Church proper they just had to obey and follow their pastors. All that has now changed. There have always been plenty of thoroughly convinced and model Catholics. But nowadays there is an increasing number who take their own initiative stemming from their deep convictions. They may even have their personal approach to the internal problems of the Church. In some countries that saw themselves as Christian and in which it was taken for granted that you just went along with the crowd, Catholics have now awakened to find in fact that they are in the minority in a non-Christian population and the Church consists now of people expressly committed to their faith. This is reflected also in the current approach to Scripture and Patristics and in ecumenical relations, all pointing to the Church less as an organised establishment than as a community of believers. And anthropology is once more being assessed in the perspective of ecclesiology.

All this has meant a revival of pneumatology, for the interior absorption of Christ in an individual is the work of the Holy Spirit. It is he who inspires responsible convictions and fosters initiative.

In the last few years this attitude has been spreading and taking on new forms. The positive aspect of this is seen in the need people feel for self-expression and airing their personal point of view, exchanging ideas and getting the feel of things for themselves. The negative aspect is a purely simplistic criticism of the establishment and total disregard for everything that is not a current innovation and in the making of which one has no hand. It is often even a vacuous mania for changing things for the sake of change or an itch for doing exactly the opposite to whatever has been handed down. And these people try to justify their behaviour by saying that they are under the influence of the Spirit who is a free agent and the source of creativity and innovation.

Oddly enough, once people of that sort start justifying themselves by reference to the Holy Spirit they take on an authoritarian stance. We noted just now that the Holy Spirit's intervention was claimed to justify the institutional image of the Church and its authority. Many of the faithful today claim the Holy Spirit as their credentials for monopolising the right to decide on their own home-made code of conduct in defiance of clergy, institution and hierarchy. For instance they are determined to decide for themselves whether they will have children anyway. And it is not just a matter of a high-handed rejection of the papal decree *Humanae Vitae* but likewise the dismissal of many a point in traditional dogmatic teaching.

We need hardly say that we are not holding up that kind of attitude as a model of pneumatology. If one made that kind of claim on the Holy Spirit we would soon need some pretty rigid rules for the discernment of spirits, indeed of the Holy Spirit! It has come to the point where the Holy Spirit is cited to justify everything and anything without rhyme or reason. And yet the attitude we have just described is a forceful factor in the prevailing climate of pneumatology. We may probe a little further into this question of pneumatology and explore the less questionable areas of it.

Here the influences at work are the study of the Bible and of the deep theological incentives of the Church of the Fathers, the impact of ecumenism and the awareness of a relatively new concept of pastoral ministry and apostolate. All this exercised considerable influence during the Council and the trend that emerged has gone on since then. We may take a look at the influence this has had on the areas with which we are concerned here.

There has been a transfer from the image of the Church as a set and unchangeable society, a kind of smooth running sacred machine, to an image of the Church as being actively and currently moulded by God. The first image has been described by Möhler as follows: "God created the hierarchy and in doing so he made ample provision for every contingency right to the end of time". That image has been superceded, as the Council has shown, in two directions: vertically by a shift of focus onto the ever present action of God and horizontally by awareness of the gifts of God traceable in all the faithful. And the reality of this horizontal aspect is due entirely to the generosity and free action of the vertical. There you have pneumatology!

It is God who constructs his Church, God who calls us (cf. Rom 1,6; People of God, Church of God: 1 Cor 1,1 and 2 Cor 1,1). It is God who distributes the gifts of service (cf. 1 Cor 12,4–11), God who gives increase (cf. 1 Cor 3,6). It is from Christ that the whole body is coordinated (cf. Eph 4,16). God has given to some to be apostles, to others teachers and prophets, each and all having their place in the Body (cf. 1 Cor 12,28). When St Paul speaks of Christ he does not describe him as the founder (the one who in the past founded and finalised a society: *societas perfecta*) but as the foundation of society (cf. 1 Cor 3,11f) here and now. That does not mean that the existing institution is not also needed but it does ward off the danger of seeing everything as nothing other than institution.

Indeed in order to build up his living Body, Christ did

not limit himself to making permanent use of visible and social means, what one might call the framework of the alliance – sacraments, apostolate and ministries established by him. For he calls on all the faithful to make their contribution by placing at the service of his work the gifts of nature and of grace which are known as charisms. As long ago as 1943 the Encyclical *Mystici Corporis*, whilst it spoke of the Holy Spirit as the interior principle of the Mystical Body, showed the role of charisms in ecclesiology. Significantly this was presented in the Encyclical's specific perspective and context, namely, the close identification of the Body of Christ with the social and hierarchical body of the Roman Catholic Church. As to Vatican Council II the perspective and context of its thinking is the People of God advancing steadily through human history towards the realities of eschatology. The Council had a great deal to say about charisms and since the Council they have been kept very much in view, precisely in recognition of their valuable contribution to ecclesiology.

The first quality brought out is the variety of gifts and their cohesion. The First Letter to the Corinthians brings this out clearly. It says: "There are varieties of working, but it is the same God who inspires them all in every one. To each is given the manifestation of the Spirit for the common good. To one is given through the Spirit the utterance of wisdom, and to another the utterance of knowledge according to the same Spirit, to another faith by the same Spirit, to another gifts of healing by the one Spirit, to another working of miracles, to another prophecy, to another the ability to distinguish between spirits, to another various kinds of tongues, to another the interpretation of tongues. All these are inspired by one and the same Spirit, who apportions to each one individually as he wills" (1 Cor 12,6–11).

It is thus God who, in the freedom of the Spirit, distributes a variety of gifts which the faithful must place at the service of one another in view of the common task of the Christian life and as a means of extending Christian influence by service to others and by bearing witness. Each and everyone must take part in this. One has only to turn to the wealth of thought in certain passages of Vatican II documents on the apostolate of the laity and on missionary activity to show how true this is. Take for instance the following from No. 3 of *Apostolate of the Laity*: "From the reception of these charisms, even the most ordinary ones, there arises for each of the faithful the right and duty of exercising them in the Church and in the world for the good of men and the development of the Church, of exercising them in the freedom of the Holy Spirit who 'breathes where he wills' (Jn 3,8), and at the same time in communion with his brothers in Christ and with his pastors especially".

This pneumatological view of the Church can be spelt out in the following five points.

1. The Church is not ready-made but is constantly moulding itself or being moulded by God. Everything is not, so to speak, handed out or "prefabricated". There is room for people to make their personal contribution to bear and exercise their creativity.

2. The fulness of the Spirit in the Church comprises the sum total of all the gifts of the Spirit with which its members are endowed. The Church is not a kind of pyramid with all the people spread out passively at its base and receiving everything from the summit. That was the concept everyone held for centuries. But the Church is a communion. It certainly has a tangible structure and it is precisely this that makes the expression "hierarchical communion" meaningful. As a tangible communion it has its requirements and its mode of self-expression. There is then no question of escaping from the realities into a theoretical idealism. Nor can there be any question of confining this communion with its wealth of reality to the patterns of thought prevalent at any given era or milieu or particular tradition or school of thought. Nor must it allow itself to drop everything and be swept off its feet by the latest way of thinking and acting that arises. It is a communion capable of a wide embrace.

It is not only in individual communities that this is discovered, thanks to the mutual recognition of the gifts with which each member is endowed. It is equally discernible in the distinctive traits acquired by today's energetic renewal, of local Churches within that wide embrace of the Church Catholic and Universal. It has been said that the Church is Catholic precisely by the virtue of its embracing, by the communion of local diverse Churches, all the particular and varied gifts which each Church has received. None can say to another, "I have no need of you" (cf. 1 Cor 12,21; compare with Rev 3,17). This point will be of particular significance in the field of ecumenism.

3. Command of situation, stability, is a quality of the spirit (the Spirit). That is why, unique and unchangeable, he can fill the universe and act deeply within each individual with total regard for his or her inner self and distinctive personality (cf. 1 Cor 2,10–11; compare with Gal 4,6: the Spirit sent into our hearts). That is the meaning the Liturgy of Pentecost had in view in applying the text of Wisdom 1,7 to the Holy Spirit. A further quality of the Spirit is freedom: see, for instance, John 3,8, 1 Corinthians 12 and 2 Corinthians 3,17. One has to recognise that certain operations are distinctive of the Holy Spirit. The term used by theologians is "by appropriation", without suggesting that the term offers a complete grasp of the reality which it covers nor that it does full justice to all that is indicated in the Scriptures. Language is inadequate in speaking of the freedom of the Spirit. Whilst taking care not to speak of the Holy Spirit as purely and simply the "vicar of Christ", a purely executive agent as it were, one cannot attribute to the Spirit and autonomy with regard to the substance of the task in hand. The Holy Spirit cannot be isolated from Christ. Christ's work is actualised by the Holy Spirit in the course of human events.

This observation has its importance when it comes to seeing where the established or ordained ministries stand with regard to the variety of charisms and the services they provide. Under the term "ministries" we can include any reliable and stable Christian service duly recognised and endorsed. But the ordained ministries, especially that of bishop and priest, designed for presiding at the Eucharist, are intimately linked to what may be aptly called the structures of the alliance, in other words, recognisably human and social realities, permanently, visibly and socially adopted and specifically designed to carry out the work of the Word Incarnate. Gotthold Hasenhüttl, a disciple of Hans Küng, has suggested that charisms provide the lines on which the Church is structured. That theory needs to be examined in the light of what we have just been saying. It is an admissible theory on condition that we are quite clear about the exact place occupied amongst the charisms or gifts of the Spirit by those which are linked with the sacrament significantly known as the sacrament of Holy Orders, which has a distinct structural function in the community (the Church). The role of the ministries brought into being by this sacrament is to signify and ensure the continuous relationship to the work of the Word Incarnate, on the one hand by assuring unity within each and every community and between communities, and on the other hand by witnessing to the unbroken link with the apostolic institution and guaranteeing its continuance. Hence the function of controlling charisms and the use made of them attributed to the Apostles and their successors by Tradition and by Vatican II.

In the same way Thomas Aquinas, having construed an impressive type of evangelism based on the doctrine of the "new law", which consists mainly of the grace of the Holy Spirit, went on to pin-point the danger arising from distorting this doctrine by recourse to make-believe, private inspiration. He said: "Men led by the Holy Spirit bow to human laws"[1]. Abuses can arise at both ends of the scale: anarchy can result from a take-over by false charismatics but equally the right to initiative can be cornered by a resurgence of legalism and clerical authoritarianism.

4. This all leads us to realise how important the action of the Holy Spirit is and to conceive a Trinitarian model of

1. *Tamen hoc ipsum est de ductu Spiritus Sancti quod legibus humanis subdantur* (Summa Theologica, Ia IIae, q.96, a.5, ad 2m).

ecclesiology. The connection between the dogma of the Holy Trinity and Christian life offers considerable scope for the theologian. Once you think of the Church on a Trinitarian model you are led to see in the nature of the Church a communion of persons, a diversity of situations and the necessity of mutual communication and exchange. In practical terms that means that the "hierarchy" must not get tied up in itself and that the action of the Spirit does not flow in one exclusive direction. The Spirit is not the monopoly of the "hierarchy" to be, as it were, controlled and released as thought fit to the lower echelons. No, the Spirit resides just as truly in the faithful and, it must be noted, the ordained ministers themselves are in the first place to be numbered among the faithful. How theologically sound St Augustine was when he insisted: "*Vobis sum episcopus, vobiscum Christianus*" ("I am a bishop for you, but a Christian along with you"). One with you I am a servant, a sinner, a sheep under the crook of the one and only Shepherd.

What Augustine was conveying was the interrelation between the representative function instituted by Christ and the personal life lived by the grace of the Holy Spirit.

5. Lastly, in the perspective of the relation between Christ and the Holy Spirit, we must examine how what has already been received from Christ is related to what is still to come. In this connection we must look at the wording of the promises made by the Lord. "I have yet many things to say to you, but you cannot hear them now. When the Spirit of truth comes, he will guide you into all the truth; for he will not speak on his own authority, but whatever he hears he will speak, and he will declare to you the things that are to come. He will glorify me, for he will take what is mine and declare it to you" (Jn 16,12–14). We discern here a kind of encounter along with continuity between what Christ said in the period before the Pasch and what the Holy Spirit will say in the period after Pentecost, a reasoning out of truth in the light of what is indentical in both cases and what is new. The two are in no way contradictory but offer, as it were, two aspects of a single reality which is none other than the history of

salvation. We would do well to dwell on this for a moment.

What Christ presents has still to come about in the course of history in a way not yet achieved. History is the unfolding of what time still holds in store. It is the epoch of the Spirit. That epoch is the same as the epoch of Christ but by virtue of the specific mission of the Spirit, consequent on the mission of Christ, it comes as the fruit of his Pasch (cf. Jn 7,39). Christ's plan is thus seen to unfold, as the writings of St John in particular so aptly express it. John shows that what Christ lived out in the "days of his flesh" (*in carne*) was to be dynamically extended into the future in the person of his disciples. This dynamism is assured by the "other Paraclete" who, as the earnest of our eschatological inheritance, constantly carries forward towards its accomplishment the life of Christ in those who are his own people, and even – though this may be stretching John's point somewhat – the overall plan of salvation throughout the world and its history. We must even broaden the field of the impact of the manifestations and operations of the Spirit to include what is called the profane world. The Fathers loved to repeat the saying of the Ambrosiaster: "*Omne verum, a quocumque dicitur, a Spiritu Sancto est*" ("Every true thing, whoever may utter it, has the Holy Spirit as its source"). The Spirit is thus seen as God giving the lead, God ever beckoning forward, God the source of renewal and of the hitherto unknown, the eschatological endowment already at work in the world's history. This was beautifully and powerfully put by Bishop Hazim, Metropolitan of Al Ladhiqiyah, in his inaugural address to the Upsala Assembly in 1968. In the Creed, he said, the Spirit is designated as "he who has spoken through the prophets". That is exactly what his specific mission is. But since the economic Trinity (that which deals with human beings and brings about their salvation: indwelling God) reveals the immanent Trinity (existing in God himself) we must in this context recognise what we have called the hypostatic mark of the Spirit in the common action of the three Persons.

72

What we have so far said is undoubtedly sufficient to alert us to the vital importance of pneumatology as an area for research. It is not something we can just take for granted. As Dietrich Bonhoeffer put it, there is a price to pay for grace. The urgency and complexity of the questions we are faced with today are motive enough for us to undertake serious theological reflections pursued in an atmosphere of prayer, by way of paying that price. In this connection we may find the Pentecostal Movement helpful to a certain extent. Setting aside the more or less spectacular show it is inclined to indulge in and its tendency to go in for experimentation and using emotion as a yardstick for fervour, the Pentecostal Movement can serve as a school for prayer. And we certainly need to practise deep prayer. The Movement may perhaps be taxed with lack of theological content — though one can also overdo preoccupation with theology — with having an itch for intimacy and advocating "privatisation" of religious living whereas today social and political implications are more usually stressed. All the same, it is good to have around a purely spiritual trend which is not shackled by preoccupations with efficiency and instant action.

A soundly balanced pneumatology, it must be noted, fully appreciates the worth of action and social initiative along with the true worth of intimately implanted religious practice and personal fervour as well as ecclesial activities.

One last point. We have been describing the chief manifestations of a new resurgence of the impact of pneumatology, especially in the life of the Church. I have barely touched on the theological or dogmatic studies which are going on at present and which are so desirable. Here are some of the topics dealt with. The Holy Spirit, principle of unity in the Mystical Body; the one and the same Spirit in Christ and in his members (this is a traditional notion in Scholastic theology and was taken up by Vatican II and mapped out in a new way by H. Mühlen); the Holy Spirit and mission; the role of the Holy Spirit in the sacraments; the Holy Spirit and the Eucharist. Finally it is surely possible to arrive at an agreement in this field between the Oriental and the Latin Traditions, provided we and they are prepared to overcome our habitual antagonisms and superficial approach towards each other. But the essential thing is that the Spirit must be present, active and a living reality in our everyday existence. Of this we must be unshakeably convinced and we must never cease imploring God to keep within us what he has promised. For in the Scriptures the Spirit is specifically designated as the promise, the earnest of our inheritance as the children of God.

Chapter 7

Theology of the Holy Spirit and Charismatic Renewal*

The theology of the Holy Spirit based on Christian experience

We are here looking at the everyday experience of countless souls. We are aware of an urge within us attracting us to the Sacred Scriptures, a love of Jesus, a desire to live in harmony with him, to be nurtured by his Eucharist, to have a growing attraction for prayer. Sometimes, however rarely, prayer wells up within us like something quite beyond ourselves. We feel a readiness to enter into communion with others despite the reticence rooted in our earthy nature. What we are then experiencing comes from the Holy Spirit. True enough it might be possible to point to psychological or physiological factors on grounds that what happens within us is traceable to elements inherent in us. Yet we firmly assert that the above experience does come from the Holy Spirit. How so? Because what is happening carries me beyond myself, even despite myself, clean contrary to the being of flesh and blood that I am and my existence in this world, on this earth. And when I line this experience up with what the Scriptures say or people of noted spiritual knowledge assert, or the saints, I realise that it is exactly that, neither more nor less than the work of the Spirit. It fits in exactly with what these sources say about the Breath of God. We recognise his fruits: peace, joy, fortitude, fulfilment. It matches the way he works, not by the constraint of law but by attraction, aspiration, response to bidding, the thing we discover supremely in the

* *La Vie Spirituelle* (September–October 1981).

75

lives of the saints. Take for instance the youthful St Theresa of Lisieux. Her doctrine and practice of it, little acts of self-sacrifice, came much less from the exercise of asceticism than from openness to sound spiritual teaching, from being inspired by love. All along it means turning away from flesh and blood propensity in us and being open instead to God, as true followers of Christ. It for that purpose that the Spirit has been given to us and is at work within us. And in this way he brings us to understand, or at least suppose, who he really is.

The Spirit formed Christ in Mary's womb. Mary by her faith was open to the Spirit's action and the Spirit activated the capacity of her feminine nature to conceive. It is the Spirit who forms Christ in us. It is he who ensures the fecundity of the Church. The account of the beginning of the Church in the Acts of the Apostles corresponds to the opening chapter of St Luke's Gospel. The Fathers and Thomas Aquinas take the terminology used at its face value. Thus they identify the "seed" by which, to quote 1 John 3,9, we are born of God with the Holy Spirit. It is true that in 1 Peter 1,23 the seed of God is identified with the "abiding word of God" received with faith. "Having purified your souls", the passage reads, "by your obedience to the truth for a sincere love of the brethren, love one another earnestly from the heart; you have been born anew, not of perishable seed but of imperishable, through the living and abiding word of God". There is no contradiction here. Faith and the Holy Spirit are constantly presented as jointly bringing about the birth and growth of Christ in us. That was so in the case of Mary (Augustine says she first conceived in her soul and then in her womb) and it is so in our case too. There is an abundance of Scripture texts bearing this fact out: "That we might receive the promise of the Spirit through faith", we read for instance in Galatians 3,14 (cf. also Gal 3,2.5 and 5,5; Eph 1,3; Acts 15,8–9 and 19,2; Jn 8,37–39). And where there is mention of unction it is that of both faith and the Holy Spirit.

Christ is the Son of God made man and the Son is ever orientated towards the Father (cf. Jn 1,1 and 14,12). "God sent his only son, born of woman, so that we might receive adoption as sons. And because you are sons, God has sent the Spirit of his Son into our hearts, crying, 'Abba! Father!' '' (Gal 4,4–6). The Spirit is the Breath, the gush of air that wafts back to the Father. "Breath" is his name. But John also calls him "living water" welling up to eternal life in God (cf. Jn 4,14 and 7,37–39). St Ignatius of Antioch gives us an inspiring account of his own experience. "My wordly desires have been crucified . . . and within me is the gentle voice of living water bidding me, 'Come, make your way to the Father' ''. This living water is the Spirit of God himself. One can only come to God by way of God. One cannot return to the Father except by welcoming the envoy he has sent us and the gift he has given us, the Son and the Holy Spirit. Of both the one and the other the Scriptures say that they have been given to us (for the Son: see Jn 3,26 and Rom 8,32) but the Spirit is the gift personally and properly so named[1]. The Holy Spirit is thus the means to an end, but a means totally identified with the end. Better still we might say the Spirit is the Reality of God's self-communication, God makes us hope for nothing less than himself and offers us in gift nothing less than himself. Thus the Holy Spirit is God hypostatised as Gift. The Holy Spirit is, in God, the consummation of communications within the Godhead, the substantial communication which has the Father as its source. This is truly fitting for God is Goodness since he is Generosity and Love, and he communicates his goodness, life and love to his creatures made in his image and likeness. We can see the same notion in St Cyril of Alexandria's remark that the perfect gift is nothing less than entering into participation with the Holy Spirit.

The Holy Spirit is in God and is for us consummation and perfection. He is, as the New Testament says, the eschatological Gift, that is, the ultimate, the absolute. St Peter sees Pentecost in the perspective of the "last days" and quotes the prophet Joel: "In the last days it shall be, God declares, that I will pour out my Spirit upon all flesh"

1. Y. Congar, *I Believe in the Holy Spirit*: Vol. 3: *The River of Life* (Seabury Press/Geoffrey Chapman).

(Acts 2,17). He is the power at work in the Kingdom of God. When Jesus cures somebody or drives out devils it is by the Holy Spirit and he declares: "The Kingdom of God has come near to you". The experience of the coming of the Holy Spirit at Pentecost came to be reiterated far and wide in the Church as one can read in the Acts and in the Letters to the Corinthians, and the Christians came to express Christ's preaching of the Kingdom in terms of the working of the Holy Spirit. They spoke of the Lord himself as acting as Spirit: "for this comes from the Lord who is the Spirit" (2 Cor 3,15–17). Several of the Greek Fathers made their own the wording of manuscripts which read, "Thy Spirit come and purify us" instead of "Thy Kingdom come", in the Our Father. The culmination of the Kingdom, beyond even the mediation of Christ, will be "that God may be everything to everyone" (1 Cor 15,28). In all the writings of St Paul these words are surely the most profound, set in a pure perspective of the infinite. All deeply religious souls have always desired that God should be everything to them, light and peace and joy, their holiness and their prayer. Serapion put it this way: "May the Lord Jesus and the Holy Spirit speak within us and may he through us sing your praises" (Anaphora 2,4). And St Theresa of Lisieux in her Act of Consecration to Love said: "O my God, be you yourself my sanctity". And in her *Story of a Soul* she wrote: "In order to love you as you love me I would need to borrow your own love". Is not that exactly what the Holy Spirit provides, so subtly and so intimately that one can no longer tell whether it is he or oneself who exclaims in prayer, "Abba! Father!"? In Galatians 4,6 it is the Holy Spirit; in Romans 8,16 it is us. But a little further on, in Romans 8,26–27, St Paul says: "We do not know how to pray as we ought, but the Spirit himself intercedes for us with sighs too deep for words. And he who searches the hearts of men knows what is in the mind of the Spirit, because the Spirit intercedes for the saints according to the will of God". That may sound incredible but it is absolutely true. Through prayer and life in the Spirit we desire with the desire of God himself. And that is not all. With Theresa of Lisieux we could quote St Augustine, William of St-Thierry, St John of the Cross, Fénelon. They would all assure us that having received the gift of the Holy Spirit we love with the very love with which God loves. And we have St Paul's word for it: "God's love (that love which is in God) has been poured into our hearts through the Holy Spirit who has been given to us"(Rom 5,5). Indeed we have the word of Jesus himself for it: "Love one another as I have loved you"; "That they may be one even as we are one"; "That the love with which you have loved me may be in them" (Jn 13,34; 17,22.26).

It seems altogether too sublime to be true! And indeed it would be if it were not the gift of God. St Augustine rightly says: "What gift might one give the person one loves if not the gift of one's very self?" "God gives nothing less than himself"; "an equivalent gift, the Holy Spirit. . ."[2]. It is an eschatological gift, that of our ultimate future. At the present time we have an earnest of it, a beginning which is of the same nature as the whole of what has been promised to us but is indeed only the beginning. It is just enough to make it possible for us to live, here in the flesh, the life of a child of God.

Since in these reflections we have been talking of the sublime, we may carry them further into an area which has been found deeply impressive. We turn to Chapter Eight of the Letter to the Romans. The Apostle is speaking about creation, the whole of creation, and says it has been "groaning in travail until now". And we too, he says, "who have the first fruits of the Spirit, groan inwardly". This passage of the Letter (vv. 18-25) occurs in a context which speaks about prayer which the Spirit utters in us. The passage and our verses fit together. Hence we see that the Spirit does not pray within us but that he groans in the world which aspires to redemption and liberation. This world prays in its own way and without realising that it is praying. But we who do know, we the knowledgeable minority, first fruits of the redeemed world, we take this groaning and give it its rightful role, we embody it in prayer, launching it into orbit. The concluding passages of

2. Y. Congar, *I Believe in the Holy Spirit*, vol 3.

the second volume of my book *I believe in the Holy Spirit* explain how one can live out day by day the doxology at the end of the Eucharistic Prayer. One might picture to oneself how the Holy Spirit gathers up, like a harvest sheaf, everything in the great wide world which is, all unconsciously, Godward and brings it to the Father in praise: "Through him (Christ), with him, in him, in the *unity of the Holy Spirit*, all glory and honour is yours almighty Father. . ." Thus our daily Mass embraces the world.

Charismatic Renewal

What then of the Charismatic Renewal? Many readers of this book undoubtedly know about it and take part in it. For those who are not familiar with it here is an introduction, though it has been made well known by a number of excellent books by Wilkerson, Ranaghan, René Laurentin, Cardinal Suenens, Monica Hébrard and others. The first step is an unconditional gift of oneself to the living Christ, with a deep sense of the radical penury of our life, an openness to the Spirit through whom the living Lord works, a child-like readiness to do whatever he wishes in us and through us, a confident placing of ourselves in the prayers of our Christian brethren visited or inhabited by the Holy Spirit. In these conditions something takes place. It does not happen on each and every occasion and there is nothing automatic about it. But lives are changed, they become stimulated in peace and joy, through a new attraction to prayer, especially prayer of praise, a new attraction for the Word of God, a calm but eager openness to others. The prayer meetings have their own particular style which one may or may not find to one's liking. And several kinds of things may occur, not only prayer and singing in "tongues" but words that may throw light on life ("prophecy") and spiritual and corporal cures.

One may well ask oneself why such things happen there and do not seem to happen elsewhere — though that assertion is highly questionable. It may reasonably be asked whether people at these gatherings are not quite simply swept along by the atmosphere of mass psychology or imitative urge. The present writer does not belong to the Renewal Movement but for all that he is convinced that he lives by the Holy Spirit who gives him an attraction for prayer and for the Word of God and readily makes his own the prayer addressed to the Holy Spirit by Simeon the New Theologian (A.D. 949 – 1022): "Come thou, only one, one who is alone, since thou canst see how alone I am . . . Come, who thyself hast become desire in me and hast made me long for thee. . .". But it might well be argued that mass psychology does not provide a totally adequate explanation of the happenings at these Renewal meetings and that we have to take into account the authentic Christian fact of a special presence and action of the Lord where there are two or three gathered in his name (Mt 18,20). There is clear witness to that in Christian writings at the time of the early martyrs. St Irenaeus in his work *Against Heretics* (III, 24) wrote: "Where the Church (*ecclesia* = assembly) is, there is also the Spirit of God, and where the Spirit of God is, there is also the Church and all grace". And St Hyppolytus in his *Apostolic Traditions* says: "Let us hasten to the assembly, where the Spirit produces fruit". The present writer takes these positive assertions as criteria.

This does not mean that I have not searching questions to put to the Renewal Movement. For instance I do not much like their use of the label "charismatic", precisely because of the importance I attach to charisms understood as talents and gifts which the Holy Spirit would have us use to build up the Body of Christ. We should be on our guard against the danger of allowing the extraordinary and the sensational and, on occasion, out-of-hand enthusiasm over some happenings or other, to lead people to identify charisms with the unusual. I do not however wish to labour this point. A more serious issue is the naivity with which some people claim to see an immediate intervention of the Holy Spirit in every imaginable occurrence. "Immediate" is the telling word. They imagine that God shows us in a flash and all-ready worked out in detail what we have to do, short-circuiting the healthy use of prudence. Hand us a text, they might say, and we will grasp its meaning instantaneously. . . For the present writer the idea of being handed a pat, personal solution on a plate without lengthy and laborious research to back it up would leave him very insecure indeed. The spiritual writers have always stressed sobriety and patient and painstaking examination. I know that there is an awareness of this in the Renewal Movement. All in all I would say that the Movement is a gift of the grace of God to the times we live in and I would like to proceed to describe, by no means exhaustively, how I see its place in the Church today.

We have known a Church that was so well organised and stable that it seemed to work spontaneously by operating a perfect "filing system" of life. That was how Protestant observers saw it. Charles Westphal told us: "You Catholics give the impression that you want to run the economy of the Holy Spirit". Please do not think that I want to attack an institution to which I have dedicated the best years of my life. Nevertheless I think that God is bidding us today to realise more fully that it is he who shapes and builds the Church. It is God, Jesus Christ, who, through the Holy Spirit, inspires activities that build up the Church which is their on-going work.[3]

God does, of course, work in and through institutions of which he himself has laid the foundations. Just look, for instance, at Baptism and the Holy Eucharist which Jesus instituted. But we also see God acting in and through people. There are, for instance, the Protestant movements that bourgeoned, especially in England, in the nineteenth century. They sprang from what was called the Awakening, associated with Wesley. They were the product of persons who were captivated by Christ and dedicated themselves to his cause with the object of converting the world to him, "in this generation" as John Mott put it. The history of this remarkable upsurge is ably described by Rouse and Neill in their book *Voluntary Movements*. "Voluntary" is the key-note. These

3. See Chapter 6, *The Spirit in action*, above.

movements did not come from existing institutions, even if they did slot into them and revitalise them, but were due to the initiative of persons who got together and produced their movement. The Renewal Movement might be seen as the same kind of thing as the Awakening though the vocabulary used by each of them differs and might well reveal a difference of concept. The Renewal Movement is not the first of its kind in the Catholic Church. Pius XII, in connection with the liturgical renewal, spoke of "the Holy Spirit wafting through the Church" (22 September 1956). The same might be said of ecumenism and other movements, but there is a clearer parallel between the Awakening or the Voluntary Movements and Charismatic Renewal, which is still less institutionalised than most of these movements. We find participants who are men and women fascinated by Jesus Christ, giving themselves to him as the living Saviour of their existence and coming together holding prayer meetings without a presiding ordained minister, and if any such minister happens to be present it is in a purely personal capacity, drawn to the living Lord like all the others there. It is true that this action of the Holy Spirit leads the participants to be people living fervent lives within the Church and concerned much more with stimulating it than with challenging it. Many a well-established group of them places itself under the bishop's scrutiny for his recognition.

The more widely the Renewal Movement spreads in our Church the more, it seems to me, it stands out as a distinctive trait of the Church of today. The Church is still the vast administrative map we have always known, all neatly squared off into areas and indeed still full of vitality. But the areas do not necessarily represent the strength they used to display. On the other hand it is marvellous to see pretty well everywhere an upsurge of the Gospel in the lives of men and women who, through the coming of the Holy Spirit, rally in various ways to the cause of Jesus Christ, the living Lord. In this way a new Church texture of real evangelical significance is being woven. But it runs the risk of not being securely knit together. A properly woven texture needs the firm interweaving of woof and warp, in the present instance, the institutional and the spontaneous, both of which are fostered by the living Lord for the self-same purpose, namely, the building up of his Body made up of human beings.

Theologically the twofold action of God for the building up of the ecclesial Body of Christ is linked with the double mission of the Son who is the Word and the Holy Spirit who is the Breath, the Wind. St Irenaeus, in his endearing genial way, imagines them as the two hands of the Father with which he moulds the human person. If we were to select just one of the many conclusions arrived at in the vast study of the Holy Spirit, I think it would have to be the recognition of the union between pneumatology and Christology, the assertion that there can be no spoken Word without the Breath and no Breath without the spoken Word. If any charismatic renewal is to be sound it must embody the Word of God, truth and doctrine. But a doctrinal statement bereft of the Breath is a dead letter. And to claim as coming from the Spirit a stimulus devoid of doctrinal content can lead to illusions, anarchy and dangerous illuminism. From the point of view of the theology of the Church, whilst recognising firmly that the Church is the living institution derived from the historical Christ, its founder, some 2000 years ago, we must also realise that it is being shaped here and now by the living Christ and Saviour who is the permanent foundation on which it rests. But the living Christ acts through his Spirit and this is so true that Christ and Spirit cannot be functionally isolated from each other. St Paul asserts this when he says the Lord *is* Spirit (cf. 2 Cor 3,17). That does not mean that St Paul fails to distinguish the two separate Persons. Indeed there are a good thirty passages about the Holy Trinity in St Paul. But when it comes to their actual operation, the Lord and the Spirit are bringing about the same thing, namely, the universal Body of Christ. The Breath is the one who breathes forth the utterance of the Word far and wide; the Spirit ensures that Christ will continue to come in Christians throughout the course of history. As time unfolds he constantly carries forward the truth which the Word contains.

Towards ecumenism

I have come back to the theology of the Third Person because it seems to me that the Renewal Movement, seen as a factor in the life of our Church, establishes an extremely important line of approach to ecumenism. After 1000 years of rupture and fifteen years of "dialogue in charity", theological dialogue began in 1981 between the Orthodox Church and the Roman Catholic Church. By great good fortune it was agreed to begin the dialogue on grounds which we clearly and profoundly hold in common, namely, the sacraments and indeed the sacramental nature of the Church. On these grounds, despite our serious divergences, we and the Orthodox are deep down one Church. For truly the Holy Catholic Church of East and West both sprang from the same roots, both recognise the same Councils and the same Fathers and have never completely broken off communion with one another. But for all that there are serious grounds of contention between the two Christian families in precisely the matter of the theology of the Spirit. The Orientals adhere literally to the New Testament formulary, "who proceeds from the Father" (Jn 15,26) and the West proclaims, "who proceeds from the Father and the Son". There is the further and by no means negligible question of the unilateral incorporation of these words in the Creed but I am leaving that aside to concentrate on the doctrinal issues as such.

I made a close study of this subject in volume 3 of *I believe in the Holy Spirit* with the sub-title "The River of life flows in the East and in the West". I have reached the conclusion, well supported if I am not mistaken by André Halleux, Louis Bouyer and Serge Boulgakov whom I intend to quote, that it is the self-same faith that is held and lived by in East and West but that the faith is spelt out in two distinct theological presentations, each comprehensive and completely structured, so much so that they cannot slot into each other. They are indeed two distinct dogmatic versions, for we at least attribute a dogmatic import to the "Filioque". This is a serious situation. What we need to do is to discover a mutually

85

adequate dogmatic pronouncement rather like the conciliation attempted at the Council of Florence in 1439, though hopefully in more promising conditions. Sound bases are to hand for such an exercise. And, once again, there is the fact that the faith practised on both sides is identical. Members of the Renewal Movement can vouch for that. Indeed we are all a living proof of that. I do not know whether the Orthodox read our spiritual writings but we certainly draw spiritual nourishment from theirs. I find myself quite at home with the writings of St Basil, St Gregory Nazianzen, Simeon the New Theologian, St Sergius and many another. And there are also others of more recent date, like Paul Evdokimov and Olivier Clément. Without wishing to appear possessive we may think of them as ours. They express and nurture our experience of the Spirit and what we believe about him. The Renewal Movement is proof enough that the same river of living water that springs from the throne of God and of the Lamb (cf. Rev 22,1) flows in both the East and West even though particular traits are discernible, just as the same kind of plant watered by a river may develop variant characteristics in different climatic conditions. Daniel-Ange has written poetry about it full of the flood of Eastern thought. Serge Boulgakov was in recent years able to make the following statement in his book on the Paraclete. He wrote: "For many a long year we have made use of all the means at our disposal to track down any influence exercised by dogmatic divergence regarding the procession of the Holy Spirit on the life and doctrine of both of the sister Churches, and we have done everything in our power to grasp exactly what it was about, what was the vital significance of the divergence and where and how it showed itself in practice. I must confess that I have not discovered any. What is more, I would quite simply assert that it does exist. When it comes down to a practical level, the two parties are unable to prove that there is any divergence between them in their veneration of the Holy Spirit despite their lack of agreement on the procession of the Third Person. It is indeed quite striking that a dogmatic divergence, seemingly so crucial, has no practical repercussion, whereas, normally, dogma always has important practical consequences and determines religious life. . . One can safely say that neither in the Oriental nor in the Western Church is there any traceable vital heresy regarding the Holy Spirit and there certainly would be if there had been any dogmatic heresy''.

Members of the Renewal Movement, and those of us who are not, live by the Holy Spirit. It is a life which envelopes theology and dogmatics. They are areas of study which have filled my years. I can safely say that I stand apart from anti-dogmatism and pragmatism but I am also aware that the formulas we have devised are not perfect. Thomas Aquinas, my master, defined dogma as *"perceptio veritatis tendens in ipsam"* (a perception of truth that leads to its embrace). In life and in spiritual experience we are brought into contact with truth, Reality itself. Or, rather, it contacts us, for we only "know" God (in the biblical sense of knowing, which implies love and familiar acquaintance) because we have first been "known" by him, that is to say, loved and reached out to by him. Imagery and formulas bearing on this are additional to it. That does not mean they are merely secondary, for they are of major importance. But it remains true that they only orientate us towards that Reality and reach out towards it.

Let us all pray earnestly that the two sister Churches, Oriental and Western, may be led by the one Spirit who dwells in them and stimulates them, to recognise that they both confess the same faith which they have received from the Apostles, the Fathers and the Councils which they both accept.

Chapter 8

The Church
as communion of faith[*]

This chapter is presented with the twofold stamp of
ecclesiology as conceived by Vatican II and ecumenism.
This is as it should be because many questions which
preoccupy us today call for a renewed vision of what it
means to live out one's existence in the Church and to do
so just at the moment when we are beginning to be able to
take these questions up without being committed to
ecclesio-centralism.

The Council set aside the image of the Church as a
predominantly juridical entity, the kind of image that sees
the Church as having produced us and we as having no
part in its shaping. Christian persons (let's say
"Consciences") have never ceased to bring something to
the life of the Church — how could it be otherwise? — but
that fact did not figure in the themes studied in
ecclesiology. In theological treatises, official documents
and even in religious instruction the Church was presented
as entirely ready-made from on high along predetermined
ways and means. By contrast the Council inserted in
ecclesiology the notions of the People of God, sacrament
(sign and means) of salvation, collegiality and co-
responsibility at every level, charisms or spiritual gifts, the
sacredness of the Christian existence of the faithful who
are engaged in mission, community liturgy, the inherent
qualities of local Churches. . . And to all that must be
addded the historical perspective, the rejection of the habit
of harking back to the Middle Ages, religious freedom in

* La Vie Spirituelle (October 1969).

88

the setting of civil legislation, the engagement of Christians in shaping world-wide society through the medium of cultures and pluralistic politics. It all adds up to an impressive programme.

Father Schillebeeckx described the novel aspect of the axis of ecclesiology envisaged by the Council thus: a vertical decentralisation orientated towards Christ; a horizontal decentralisation of Rome towards the universal episcopacy and of the hierarchical ministry towards the People of God; of the Roman Catholic Church towards the other Churches and lastly the giving up of a certain ecclesio-centralism[1]. That is indeed an accurate description. And it is in that framework that we would like to situate and develop our present reflections and in doing so to show the very real coherence, logic and basic unity of the two decentralisations, making full use of the New Testament notion of communion.

Our starting point is the clear-cut affirmation that it is the Lord who shapes his Church. The Church is a posited institution, at least as regards its principles, following on the Incarnation. But is also a happening. That is surely the point the Liturgy is making in choosing the episode of Zacchaeus (Lk 19,1 – 10) as the Gospel for the feast of the Dedication of a church, a feast which exudes ecclesiology! Zacchaeus was not identifiable with religious officialdom but Christ gave him recognition, chose him and called him. Zacchaeus received him in his house. The fact that Jesus goes there and is welcomed there has the effect of bringing salvation to that house. There we have a "happening". If we were to set about formulating a complete theology of the Church we would also have to take into account Pentecost and the initiatives taken by the Holy Spirit. In our present reflections we are presuming that the reader is familiar with that theology.

The Lord and the Holy Spirit build up the Church by bringing many a Zacchaeus to share in countless ways in the goodness of the Lord and the Holy Spirit. That is precisely where the New Testament notion of communion, *koinonia* in Greek, comes into play.

---

1. E. Schillebeeckx, *L'Église du Christ et l'homme d'aujourd'hui selon Vatican II* (Mappus 1965).

The Church as communion and fraternity

God, wrote St Paul to the Corinthians (who were well and truly of the Zacchaeus type), has called us into communion ("fellowship", the Revised Standard Version of the Bible renders it) with his Son Jesus Christ our Lord (cf. 1 Cor 1,9). The word for "called" (*convocatus*), be it noted, is of the same etymology as the word for Church, which is "convocation", that is, the assembly of those who are called to share in Jesus Christ. And again in the closing lines of the second letter (2 Cor 13,14) St Paul wished the Corinthians "communion (fellowship) of the Holy Spirit". This prepares for the message of the Apostle John. He spells out what the Apostles have handed on or communicated. It is nothing less than the living truth (life-and-truth) which dwelt with the Father and manifested itself in Jesus Christ. As a result the faithful can have communion, "fellowship" with the Father and with his Son, Jesus Christ (cf. Jn 1,1–3). But this fellowship and communion, if it is genuine, that is, if it leads us to walk in the light, brings us into communion, that is to say, unity and sharing, with one another. "If we walk in the light as he (God) is in the light we have fellowship with one another" (1 Jn 1,6–7). That then is the logical pattern and the scope of this communion and fellowship. It is a sharing in one and the same Reality, namely, God the Father, Son and Holy Spirit, generating unity among those who, sharing the same God, are pledged and led to share in fellowship what they themselves possess.

The Reality in which we share and which is the source of our common life is variously designated as salvation (cf. Jude 3), Gospel (cf. Phil 1,5), faith (cf. Tit 1,4 and Philem 6) and participation in the Body and Blood of Christ shared in the Cup and the Breaking of bread (cf. 1 Cor 10,16).

That the logical consequence of this communion for us is a communion comprising community of goods and sharing of them is borne out by the New Testament use of the word *koinonia*. It conveys the notion of sharing things necessary for everyday material existence (cf. Heb 13,16;

90

Acts 2,44 and 4,32) and, in St Paul, the relief-funds raised and which, as the Letters show, had striking ecclesial significance (cf. 2 Cor 8,3–4 and 9,12–13; Rom 12,12 and 15,26–27). It was a kind of sacrament, a sign and a means of unity between the Christians converted among the Gentiles and the "saints" of Jerusalem. We detect it in the scene when James, Cephas and John, "the pillars", gave Paul, the new Apostle, the hand of fellowship (cf. Gal 2,9–10) and established a kind of convention between him and them. And there is the indication (cf. Gal 6,6) that the disciple should share his material possessions with the one who has taught him the word of God.

This all shows that there is no union with God without fraternal relations sharing and community. The Lord builds up his Church by calling to himself and giving each person gifts which, as far as can be, must be shared with everyone else. When Zacchaeus received the visit of the Lord he understood there and then that he had to not only restore four-fold what he had extorted from others but also to distribute half of his possessions to the poor. Sharing the same life, the same faith, the same baptism, the same Bread, "we are one Body of Christ and individually members of one another, having gifts that differ according to the grace given us" (Rom 12,5–6) and therefore we must "As each has received a gift employ it for one another as good stewards of God's varied grace" (1 Pet 4,10). We ought here to quote Ephesians 4,7ff and the whole of 1 Cor 12,4–11. There are many gifts "but it is the same God who inspires them all in everyone. To each is given the manifestation of the Spirit for the common good. To one is given one thing, to another another". There cannot be the slightest doubt, the Church is built up with gifts that come down to persons (vertically) so that they shall share them (horizontally) and thus all other people may benefit from them in the measure in which the Lord wishes them so to do. We receive in order that we may give. "Life has taught me that in this world you will not experience consolation unless you have first consoled others, that we receive nothing that we have not first given to others. Our human relationships are all about mutual exchange, only God, himself alone, gives" (G. Bernanos, *Les Enfants humiliés*).

The Council has placed charisms in their proper niche. They are not necessarily spectacular or exceptional gifts, quasi-miraculous phenomena. In liturgical texts the word "charism" is used in its quite ordinary meaning, simply a natural or supernatural gift which becomes apparent and is meant to help build up the community. Charisms are quite tangible realities and if the word pretty well dropped out of usage it was allegedly because it was ousted by the increasing concentration on the theology of grace.

All growth towards the fulness of the Lord's grace is precisely conditioned by the charismatic life. We must see how that growth is produced. First of all, grace engenders a new life in both the individual and the community. For grace is never given globally to a mass of people but always to one or another individual person under the form of specific charism (cf. Rom 12,3 and 6). That is why each baptised person is absolutely irreplaceable and indispensable. But at the same time we note that all the important charismatic texts point to the very image of the Body of Christ. The self-same grace that fosters individuality also serves to incorporate into the community. The Christian, because he or she is a member of the community, cannot live just for himself or herself alone, wrapped up in his or her own personal growth and refusing to contribute to the mutual building up of the community. Furthermore, grace assigns to each and everyone of us the place assigned to us individually by the will of God, whilst at the same time allowing each of us individually to expand beyond our natural limitations. Grace restrains our all too human urge for self-aggrandizement and confers that humility which enables us to be content to serve in a modest capacity.

What does all this add up to when it comes down to the practical level of ecclesiastical life? Organically that life is a single entity but within it one can distinguish elements that come from sharing and mutual use of spiritual gifts. These factors come by way of both the horizontal dimension and the vertical historical dimension.

Horizontal dimension

Our horizon is the Church here and now stretching out all around in its catholicity. Seen thus it is a network of impacts and exchanges. The texture of the Church is woven from them as well as from the sacramental and extra-sacramental graces received from God all the time. Everyone surely knows what it means to be edified (that is, spiritually built up) by the example of a mother, a fellow-worker or a friend, or to have received light, encouragement or consolation from a word someone says or a letter they write, sometimes quite unexpectedly. And we know too what it means to have our own prayers supported by those of a fervent community.

At the present time, however, the personal edification (building up) brought to us by our brethren takes more specific forms. First of all there is a broadening of the range of sources. For us the Church is the Catholic Church, but we gladly acknowledge that we are constantly receiving a great deal from our Orthodox, Protestant and Anglican fellow-Christians. Their understanding of the mystery of Christ is enriching, the witness they bear is encouraging, praying with them radiates fulfilment and peace. Meanwhile in the Catholic Church nourishing fare is laid out for us. There is the review of life, Catholic Action and *aggiornamento* of religious communities. There are stimulating exemplary cases which transpire in the course of surveys. We have in mind in particular the ones that have been brought to light by enclosed orders. There is the joint study of problems and projects. And lastly there are the evangelical groups, family groupings thanks to which the very texture of Christian life is being renewed, penetrating right into their everyday down-to-earth existence and largely responsible for bringing the Church, so to speak, a breath of fresh air.

So it is that we constantly experience what St Paul told the Christians at Rome about his only feeling: "I long to see you, that I may impart to you some spiritual gift to strengthen you, that is, that we may be mutually encouraged by each other's faith, both yours and mine"

93

(Rom 1,11–12). That grace-laden experience is all the more called for today because many people are finding themselves unable to retake their stand in the faith without the stimulus that comes from the good example given them by others, who, weak though they too may be in isolation, find strength in mutual support. "A three-fold cord is not quickly broken", says Ecclesiastes (4,12).

Without dwelling further on the spiritual benefits that one can derive individually from this mutual sharing and exchange, we would like to list briefly five aspects of it that have a bearing on ecclesiology and therefore affect the image we have of the Church. Looking beyond the exaggeratedly formal type of unit which, anyway, might fail to ring true, there is the creation of communities within which people can learn a truly healthy pluralism. The Church's structures of faith, sacraments and ministry lose nothing of their value but become more deeply interiorised. Ecclesial cohesion is secured less by a sense of legislative safeguards than by an atmosphere of communion of persons. Parallel to this, in the research regarding truths and in the declaration of them, there is greater emphasis on mutual communication, active participation and control, linked with a maturing of conscience thanks to the collaboration of an entire group. Anyone who has had experience of that kind of approach to Christian realities is left in no doubt that it affords a channel for the Holy Spirit. This, of course, presupposes that one's passion for truth is not geared to what W. G. Ward called "breakfast dogma" (as though a papal decree landed each morning on your breakfast table!), looking for a constant stream of authoritative decisions descending like dictates on people devoid of any capacity for personal responsibility. Maurice Blondel realised that deep down in the so-called integrist or reaction theory there is a concept of intellect and perception and therefore of the discovery of truth. The spiritual contributions brought by individuals play an active role in the spiritual maternity of the Church especially in so far as they become an integral part of the community which they help to form but which transcends them, taking them into itself. A community enriched by the shared life of its members is highly attractive and productive. Made up of Christians it goes on to produce Christians. Lastly, there is a kind of affinity, a kind of convergence, between that type of ecclesial life and ecumenism. Besides, in both these areas the Lord and his Holy Spirit foster a fulness of unity through the impact people make on the Churches by means of the gifts they have received.

Vertical or historical dimension

It is not only with my brethren of today that I find myself in communion. It is not only from the God-given gifts of the people actually around me that I benefit. I am a fellow-disciple of that "cloud of witnesses" with which, as the Letter to the Hebrew says (12,1), "we are surrounded". One could never possibly list them all. There are whole collections of texts and books, ancient and modern. There are names like Athanasius, Newman, Augustine, Tauler, Theresa of Lisieux. The "bread" which they received with which to nourish the Church is still there for us in what they have given to the Church. And out and beyond them and with them we share in the cloud of biblical witnesses. I find my nourishment in the faith of Abraham, I am strengthened and give voice to my fervour in the psalms of David. The breath of the prophets urges me on. And how indescribable the stimulus of the Gospels, the writings of St Paul, and our wonderful John! I never tire of reliving the experience of Abercius of Hierapolis (ca. A.D. 200) which he described in his own epitaph. It runs, "I am the disciple of the Shepherd who pastures his flock on hill and plain with eyes ever watching over one and all. It is he who gives me clear and true learning. It is he who sent me to Rome to contemplate the queen draped in golden robes. There I saw a people marked with a shining seal. I have seen, too, the plain of Syria and all its cities, and Nisibia beyond the Euphrates. And everywhere I have found myself in the company of my brethren. I had Paul for a companion. And wherever I went it was the faith that led me on. Everywhere faith gave me to drink from a vast and limpid source, drawn from it with pure, unsullied hands. Faith gave food to us friends unceasingly, and rare wine, and, withal, bread to eat. . .". Written works and formulas and sacred rites all serve to make time stand still and hold these treasures ever present. They make it possible for me to live out for myself, in company with those who have gone before us, an experience of the self-same realities as they, a participation which enriches me with all that the Spirit of the Lord wrought in them and through them. What a tremendous inheritance this is! No prince was ever bequeathed such wealth!

There is something analogous here to the handing down of culture in terms of an inheritance proudly stored up across the centuries. It is not just a stream carrying down the ages the achievements of great masters of literature and scientists and artists and musicians all jostled together. Each of them plunges into the single ever-widening stream but loses nothing of their distinctive personal traits. You can pick out each of them from that single stream with their individual style and cast of mind and the characteristics of the sources from which they came. Pluralism is not simply the product of two utterly extreme positions. It is to be found as an incalculable wealth in all the elements which, in Christianity and Catholicity, go to make up that special inheritance of culture which we know as Tradition.

We note that, thanks to the present climate of ecumenism, Protestantism has abandoned in this respect its former negative and purely polemical attitude. The starting point of the Faith and Order Conference at Montreal in July 1963 was the distinction between Tradition and traditions. By Tradition is meant the handing down to us of the mystery of Christ, whereas traditions are particular forms which this transmission has taken in the Churches, the various ways in which the one unique mystery of Christ is lived out, celebrated, given expression in various Christian groupings or "families".

This is a perfectly objective distinction resting on tangible facts, but it only really works if we hold together two quite distinct things which are both part and parcel of our notion of Catholic ecclesial Tradition. Thus we can link Tradition with vertical communication and traditions with mutual exchanges at the horizontal level. Exchanges take place between us precisely because we all share in the one same life of the Lord and his Spirit. But the traditions are simply a collected treasure-store of the impacts and exchanges achieved through persons and perceptions in a given particular cultural milieu or historical setting. Thus the traditions only exist in function of Tradition. The two are quite distinct but they must go hand in hand. At the level of the Scriptures and even regarding the "four-branched" Gospel, Tradition only reaches us by way of traditions. No need to be taken aback by that statement since we can truly say, as we have already shown, that the gift of God is both single and multiple, being given to persons and being communicated by human persons who are called to draw all together, transcending the plurality yet proceeding by means of that plurality and making unstinted use of it. God's plan proceeds one by one by means of plurality, what the writer Vladimir Soloviev calls the ideal of "unitotality". Catholicity begins in Christ the Source and proceeds to Christ the Ultimate End, the Alpha and Omega, and embraces all the works accomplished by the Holy Spirit in and through people, in and through human communities and the Church. Tradition is not only Pureness but also Plenitude, in the Body of Christ, "the fulness of him who fills all in all" (Eph 1,23).

Chapter 9

Cult, Sacrament
and preaching of the Word*

The opposition between a Church of the Word (Protestant) and a Church of the Sacraments (Catholic) is surely a thing of the past as is also the idea of attributing the efficacy of grace to the spoken Word through the Scriptures, and to the sacraments through the Church. The liturgical movement in various countries, supported by a biblical movement and often bolstered by a new approach to preaching and catechesis, has gradually led to linking the celebration of the sacraments with the preaching of the Word.

I. WORD AND SACRAMENT
IN THE THEOLOGY OF VATICAN II

The Second Vatican Council set its seal on this trend not only by its Constitution on the Liturgy but also by what it teaches about the priesthood of bishops and priests and the catechumenate as seen in missionary activity. Four points stand out in this connection in the work of the Council.

1. The Council asserts that all communication conducive to salvation has Christ as its supreme and primary source. Linked with this is the account of the different ways in which Christ is present (cf. Constitution on the Liturgy, No. 7) and that, although each of these ways is clearly distinct, they must not be isolated one from

* *Concilium* (1968).

98

another since they are ways in which the one and only Lord is present and acts and this with a single end in view, namely, the full achievement of the new and everlasting covenant.

2. The Council presents the spoken word as an integral element of the Liturgy[1] as well as of the definition of the priesthood of both bishops and priests. We shall see later on what this entails in drawing up the definition of the priestly ministry itself. But we may note here and now that it is not just a matter of increasing the use of the spoken word in liturgical celebrations, not therefore a question of quantity but of the very nature and constituent elements of the Liturgy.

3. There is the recognition that the very notion of Christian Liturgy and cult contains a specifically biblical trait which the Encyclical *Mediator Dei* had already taken up, namely, that prior to being a means for us to approach God (adoration, offering, praise, thanksgiving) Christian Liturgy or cult is the reception by us of the gift God gives us in and through Christ. But since the divine Word made himself not only the spoken word but also flesh and this *incarnation* is deep down the basis of the order of sacramental signs, it follows that a) in the Bible the aspect of efficacious action and the aspect of conveying knowledge and awareness are inseparably contained in the term "word" (in Hebrew, *dabar*); b) the word of God used as such in the Church precisely by virtue of being the word of God is also *opus Dei*, a notion worked out by J. Betz and O. Semmelroth. Most Catholic theologians nowadays recognise that the word of God has a certain sacramental structure because it has an outward sign by which the God of grace works with a view to our salvation. It is true that the effective acquiring of grace is less certain and more dependent on the minister than in the case of the sacraments properly so called and in which Christ alone operates.

4. The Council has renewed our vision of the Church, especially in speaking of it as the People of God and the universal sacrament of salvation. Without identifying

1. See especially, *Sacred Liturgy*, Nos. 6, 35 and 56.

itself with any one particular theological school of thought the Council made its own the notion of the general sacramentality of the Church. It is interesting to note as the Protestant theologian, J. Von Allmen, put it, that at times when the Church has not been particularly conscious of having to face up to the world that surrounds it and being challenged to engage in active mission to it, the trend has been to be absorbed in the thought of the sacraments rather than being conscious of the Church as sacrament. By contrast, when there is an overall sense of involvement in mission and therefore the outlook is geared to the fulfilment of the history of salvation, the focal point is Christ as the sacrament of God (what St Paul understood by his use of the word "mystery") and the Church as the sacrament of Christ. Of course one must never lose sight of the clear position of the seven sacraments as such. But for all that one must not limit oneself to them to the total neglect of the all-pervading sacramental reality of Christ and all that he enacts in and through the Church to our sanctification and to the glory of God. In this perspective the word takes its rightful place alongside the sacraments. The truly beautiful term "mystery" is much more comprehensive than the word "sacrament", which has been in general use in the West, for it comprises the two-fold aspect of knowledge and action, of the faith professed and lived by, and the celebration of the realities from which our salvation stems.

II. THE CONCEPT OF CHRISTIAN WORSHIP

All this rules out any suggestion of dichotomy between liturgical worship or sacrament and the proclamation of the word of God. This undeniable fact is borne out by a searching analysis of the notion of worship, not just as a general term but in specific terms of Christian Liturgy. It has three distinctive traits.

100

1. Christian worship as a living anamnesis

The Jews saw their worship not only as calling to mind but as actually making present the deeds of God whereby he has intervened to establish an alliance with us in order to save us. The technical term is *"anamnesis"*: remembrance which makes past events present. The Israelites came into contact with peoples practising naturalist forms of worship. Some of them were the inhabitants of countries occupied by Israel, but the Israelites, although they were sometimes tempted to adopt elements from their worship, were careful not to merge with them. The clear difference between Israel's concept of worship and that of these peoples was that the worship practised by the Jewish people was a celebration of the great deeds, the *magnalia Dei*, by which Yahweh had declared himself their God and made them his people − the deliverance from slavery, the Passover, the gifts of the Law (Pentecost), the bond of alliance, etc. All this is constantly celebrated in the psalms and they − it will be remembered − are the basis of our liturgical prayer. Exegetical studies have shown conclusively that this is indeed not just a celebration that merely calls to mind divine deeds but does actually make them present and operative. For once divine deeds have been enacted they never lose their effective value for the faithful right down the ages, and whenever the faithful celebrate them in faith and thanksgiving they make them a present, effective reality through the Holy Spirit.

Christians see a typological significance in the *magnalia Dei* of the Old Testament but over and above them comes Jesus Christ and all he is and all he has done: his Incarnation, baptism, fast, ministry, his Passion and his Resurrection followed by Pentecost, all of them celebrated year by year in the round of the calendar of the Liturgy and every single day in the Eucharist. One can see this in the prayer *Unde et memores* ("Father, we celebrate the memory . . .") in Eucharistic Prayer I. The unique historical events are thus made present and operative in the natural cycle of the seasons. Each and every one of the sacraments refers back to the Pasch of the Lord, his Passion and Resurrection, and it is these that the sacraments bring into the major decisive moments of human life. For the Eucharist links them all together since it is the celebration of that very Pasch of Christ and the New Alliance sealed in his blood.

So in the Liturgy, as the Council's Constitution on the Sacred Liturgy (Nos 33 and 35) puts it, God speaks to his people and proclaims anew the Gospel. This is ensured by the voice and actions of the Liturgy. It was always so and it is more effectively assured now that the *anaphora* is spoken in the everyday language of the local people. Thus the Mass is now clearly a proclaiming of the death of the Lord until he comes (cf. 1 Cor 11,26), whereas until this practice was introduced, only the teaching part of the Mass was in the vernacular and the "sacred mysteries" part was shrouded in Latin which the vast majority of the people did not understand. Vatican II unified the two parts of the Mass by using the vernacular throughout. The Liturgy, by word and action, surpasses anything the most authoritative and impressive sermon could achieve. That is why Pius XI could say that the Liturgy is the Church's greatest means of communication both in teaching and in fostering the faith.

But two things are worth noting. First, the names habitually given to the sacraments, like Anointing of the sick, rather obscure the unique significance which they enshrine and which they are meant to convey. Secondly, in the past no variants to the shape of the Liturgy and the liturgical texts were allowed, whatever the circumstances or the people involved, whether they were celebrating some happy occasion or were weighed down with grief, in a position of power or underdogs, children or adults, rough and ready folk or highly cultured. There was a gap in the much needed adaptation to the types and needs of the people. The celebration of the Liturgy all needed to be spelt out with that in view. This has now been provided for by the inclusion of a homily which, according to Vatican II's document *Sacrosanctum Concilium* (No. 52), must always be inserted in the public celebration and only omitted for serious reasons. The document also says that the celebration of the other sacraments should be framed in such a way as to be readily comprehensible and that some explanation should be given either before or during the celebration. The new forms we now have aim at ensuring active sharing by those present in the action of the Liturgy instead of simply witnessing what is being done. That is where the explanatory homily comes in and is foreseen as an integral part of the Liturgy (*Sacred Liturgy*, Nos 35, 52, 56).

2. Sacraments of faith

All ritual worship is a means of expressing convictions regarding a transcendent and invisible Being and in this sense may be aptly defined as a witness to faith. In pagan rites, however, the word "faith" is used in a greatly reduced analogical sense or simply points to a psychological phenomenon and does not in the least suggest a faith given by the action of God who takes initiative with regard to me because he wishes to establish a personal relationship with me. Far from being that, the pagan rites belong to a religion which is out to win the favours of a personified force of nature. In the (Juadeo–)Christian religion the medium and point of encounter with God is the history of the initiatives taken by the living God. It is a religion that belongs within a faith thanks to which I am linked to those initiatives and draw to myself the benefits they offer. Faith is my response to the action of the living God which is brought to me by his living word. It is indeed emphatically true to say that Christian worship is a determined and explicit witness of faith. That, incidentally, is how Thomas Aquinas presents it: *protestatio fidei*.

Another expression of which Aquinas is particularly fond and which was already in use in his day, is *sacramenta fidei*, sacraments of faith, which he uses whenever he speaks of the sacraments. Vatican II's *Sacrosanctum Concilium* explains the meaning of that expression when it says: "The sacraments not only

103

presuppose faith but by words and objects they also nourish, strengthen, and express it" (No. 59). In other words, faith and the sacraments (or Liturgy) are inextricably intertwined in a process in which faith is the forerunner of the ritual celebration, then runs on right through it, is given expression in it and emerges strengthened and enriched.

Theology tells us that the sacraments draw their efficacity from the Pasch of Christ, but for that they must be linked with it, not only be the fact of having been instituted by Christ but also through faith. For it is faith that provides the salvific contact. This fact is clearly brought out in the account of the woman in Matthew 9,20–21, Mark 5,25–34 and Luke 8,43–48. There we see Christ with a dense crowd pressing round him and yet just one woman in the crowd spoken of as explicitly touching him, precisely because she reached out to him with faith. St Augustine makes a point of this fact in quoting this Gospel episode and St Thomas Aquinas constantly sees faith as the means by which the necessary contact is established whereby the Passion of Christ is effectively applied to us for our benefit. That is what St Thomas has in mind when he declares that "all sacraments derive their efficacity from faith" (*"Omnia sacramenta ex fide efficaciam habent"*). How can we pinpoint this faith? Essentially it is the faith of the Church as such. The minister of the sacrament is the channel of that faith. Of course as far as validity of a sacrament is concerned all that is needed is for the minister to adhere to that faith by his intention of "doing what the Church does". But it is clear that in view of the building up of the Body of Christ in the individual members of the Church and in the community as a whole, the faith of the minister visibly evident in his stance and manner of doing the actions and saying the words of the Liturgy counts enormously. For the priest is not only a representative of the Church but also exercises a spiritual paternity by the impact of his faith and his speech. His faith is not only a personal matter, for others find a support in his faith and are nurtured by it. And the faith of the people also plays a part in the sacramental process. It does not of course *constitute* the sacrament as does the faith of the Church (though the penitent's faith comes into the sacrament of penance) but it does put the people in the right conditions for a worthy reception of the sacrament and for drawing spiritual benefit from it. In this respect the faith of the people is interwoven with the sacrament which they receive. It predisposes them by nurturing their desire to receive it and by opening their hearts and minds to Christ's grace. It helps them during the actual sacramental rite to participate fully by grasping its spiritual meaning. It helps them after the reception of the sacrament truly and consciously to make their own the fruit it offers. In the case of the Eucharist, for instance, faith will lead them to the *manducatio spiritualis*, the spiritual nourishment as a consequence of the *manducatio sacramentalis*, the consuming of the Sacred Host. But as an aid to this there is a kind of interplay, something like the affective experience that happens in our lives, whereby the clear, effective perception of the sacrament brings support to the recipient. Thanks to faith we draw benefit from a sacrament but faith itself is nurtured by the sacrament. And this cycle of interplay goes on all the time.

But since faith is thus intertwined in the sacramental rites, the more enlightened that faith is the better for those who are taking part. That is why it is of capital importance to incorporate a clear explanatory text in the rite. The Liturgy itself consists of words and gestures. It thus of itself ensures that nurturing of faith and focussing of attention on the meaning of the particular rite in hand. But, as we have said, the rite as it stands in the liturgical books runs the risk of being too impersonal and people need to be given additional guidance. One has only to think of the priest as minister of the sacrament of penance and how within the rite addressed to every penitent he strikes a personal note in what he says to each successive one.

3. *The Christian's spiritual offering of life*

Christian cult is a spiritual cult. It is, of course, involved in the handling of the material world and is concerned with our body and all our senses. So if it is spiritual that is not through being disembodied but because the spiritual constitutes its principal content. It does not consist in things but in a deep down personal union of the human person with God through faith and love. The Gospel resumes the message of the prophets regarding the primacy of the offering of ourselves to God in filial and loving obedience. The New Testament speaks of presenting our bodies as living sacrifice, holy and acceptable to God (cf. Rom 12,1; 1 Pt 2,5; Heb 9,14). To this it adds the sacrifice of praise (cf. Heb 13,15) and that of good works and sharing, "for such sacrifices are pleasing to God" (Heb 13,16). Paul himself celebrated the Christian cult in leading people to obedience in faith (cf. Rom 1,9–15.16 and Phil 2,17). And Vatican II takes up his apostolic teaching in what it says about the spiritual priesthood of the faithful in *Lumen Gentium* (No. 34) where we read: "For all their works, prayers and apostolic undertakings, family and married life, daily work, relaxations of mind and body, if these are accomplished in the Spirit become spiritual sacrifices".

The Christian cult does not consist of the objects used nor the ceremonies as such but in the relationship of himself towards God, and therefore it can only be achieved through dependence on Christ and his perfect filial relationship to God and indeed in its highest expression in his dolorous blessed Passion. And indeed that filial relationship and that self-offering and that sacrifice are all given to us so that we may unite ourselves with them, not just as a memory and a model but in their bodily reality in the celebration of the Eucharist. It follows that the Christian cult will consist in very truth in receiving with thanksgiving this gift which God gives us and in joining to it the spiritual offering of our life in all its reality. That is why priests are not just ordained to "say Mass" but to bring the faithful into communion with the cult of Jesus Christ whose "memorial" they make and whom they celebrate sacramentally. That is exactly what Vatican II teaches in *Lumen Gentium* (No. 28) and

Presbyterorum Ordinis (Nos. 2 and 5). This follows from the very nature of the sacraments and it demands of the celebrating priest something more than the performance of the rite. True enough, there are many ways of linking the sacramental celebration with the life of the people which is to be offered as their spiritual sacrifice. The entire atmosphere of the parish can be made to serve this purpose: the singing, the notices, the parish newsletter and, first and foremost, catechetical instruction. But it is specifically the homily that must come into play here (true, it has other purposes also, e.g. instruction) and it does not have to be lengthy in order to be effective.

Taken as an integral part of the Liturgy preaching is undoubtedly meant to be a commentary on the particular mystery of our faith that is being celebrated at the particular point in the liturgical calendar. But it must also help the faithful to unite their lives as an offering with Christ's own sacrifice. When we say "their lives" we do not mean a kind of meaningless framework, a kind of purely theoretical spiritual life or a routine devoid of personal involvement. What we mean is life intimately woven with events large and small and consciously intertwined with the everyday setting of daily occupations. The explanation of the liturgical texts given by the priest during the celebration helps the people to understand the mystery in the day's Liturgy but it is also meant to involve them in the celebration by making them see their life in a new light and thus bringing them to unite it with that sacred mystery. If the preaching is with this in view it will truly be a call that brings a response.

III. TWO APPLICATIONS

1. The theological notion of priesthood

The first of our applications concerns the notion of priesthood itself. On several occasions Vatican II uses the expression "*veri sacerdotes Novi Testamenti*". In doing so the Council is discreetly playing down the long-standing custom of associating our ministerial priesthood with that of Aaron. It is characteristic of the New Testament that, by contrast with the Old Testament, the sacrificial (sacerdotal) function and the prophetic function are merged and likewise synagogue (place of divine praise and teaching) and Temple become one thing in our churches. St Thomas explains that this comes about quite simply because the sacrifice we offer is a spiritual one. To put it another way, the sacrifice of the New Testament is prophetic; the cult it celebrates is worship in faith. That is why Vatican II, having incorporated preaching in the liturgical rite, has by the same token expanded the definition of the ministerial priesthood as only linked with the offering of the Eucharistic sacrifice. It has presented the image of the priest as having the spoken word as his prior concern after the manner of the Apostles and in cooperation with the bishops (cf. *Presbyterorum Ordinis*, No. 2, along with Rom 15,16)[2]. We should hold on to that perspective to get a fresh view of the priesthood as seen in the Gospel. And furthermore, since the Council envisages priestly formation as an on-going exercise, we should bear in mind the effort constantly demanded of us to gear ourselves to the world we live in so as to be men and women capable of awakening people to their faith and instruct them in it. Many a citation from by-gone authors, like Humbert (13th century), St Bernardino of Siena (15th century) and John Eck (16th century), comes to mind in this connection. For instance: "If in a given country Mass was celebrated for thirty years without any preaching and in another country there was preaching for thirty years but no Mass, the people in the second would be more solidly Christian than in the first".

2. The Decree goes on (No. 4) to speak of the priest as the minister of the Word of God and says: "In the Christian community itself, especially among those who seem to understand or believe little of what they practise, the preaching of the Word is needed for the very administration of the sacraments. For these are sacraments of faith, and faith is born of the Word and nourished by it. Such is especially true of the Liturgy of the Word during the celebration of Mass. In this celebration, the proclamation of the death and resurrection of the Lord is inseparably joined to the response of the people who hear, and to the very offering whereby Christ ratified the New Testament in his blood. The faithful share in this offering both by their prayers and by their recognition of the sacrament for what it is." (W. M. Abbott, *The Documents of Vatican II*, G. Chapman).

108

2. The importance of signs and gestures

The second application concerns pastoral ministry even more specifically. However important preaching may be you clearly cannot make people into good Christians by preaching alone. The great educationalist St John Baptist de la Salle always insisted on linking liturgical celebration with instruction in the education of children. Objects used, gestures, signs are all powerful tools for education. The point is that human beings are both body and mind. Truth is therefore not fully driven home unless it penetrates bodywise. That too is why a sacrament is more complete than a simple spiritual link with a mystery. Christ himself is not only the Word sent to the world by the Father but the body immolated and given to us. It would therefore be a distinct advantage to take a look at our store of theology together with local practices that strike a note with it and make a careful selection of a limited number of "gestures" capable of bringing home to people the basic perspectives of Christian life. It would provide a pattern on which genuine Christians could be moulded.

Chapter 10

The liturgical assembly*

Terminology

In the expression "liturgical assembly" it is the word "liturgical" that is operative. But, first, not every group of people can be called an assembly. For that, the people have to be notified of the gathering and have responded to being convoked. Furthermore, an assembly has a definite motivation, an objective to be pursued together. The objective here is the cult rendered to God by the communal Body of Christ whilst deriving a personal benefit regarding spiritual life. That cult does not rest purely on our personal initiative but comes from Christ, from his Body. We are convoked and invited to enter into it, to become members of it.

It is because this is the assembly of Christ and of his Body that it is rightly called liturgical. *Leiturgia* means "public service". Not every act of worship is liturgical. It supposes a certain public character and not just something private. And this in turn springs from two factors: it has to be an "institution" resting on the intervention of a public authority, and it has to be the prayer of an *ecclesia*, that is to say, of a community bearing the character of a Church. J. A. Jungmann gives priority to the necessity of the character of Church; A. G. Martimort to the institutional and juridical factor. The present writer finds that the Church factor is the more specific. It is indeed the more traditional one if you take into account the real meaning of ancient tradition according to which liturgical assembly and Church were clearly one and the same thing. It was by virtue of being the local Church that a given

* *La Maison-Dieu* (1973).

community carried out the *liturgical* prayer without having to have received delegation from higher authority. That is an important point but it does not entirely rule out the option of the institutional and juridical factor. Indeed we can only really speak of a Church, be it a local Church, if the group in question complies with certain essential traits, in particular that it has been convoked. A purely spontaneous association will not do. It has to be such that it is recognised by other "Churches" and that it complies with the essence of the total Church. It has to be constituted as to comprise at least an elementary form, clearly differentiated functions and a publicly acknowledged presidency. In other words, for it to be a "Church" it must have an institutional character and not just be a do-it-yourself get-together of the faithful. It follows that when the public cult of a Church is designated as liturgical the aspect of institution by authority comes in. It is a cult which is situated, by virtue of a juridical format, in an ecclesial context which stamps its authenticity on it.

Having said all this we must add that, if it is indeed in its liturgical cult (cf. *Sacrosanctum Concilium*, No. 2) that the Church is seen at its highest expression, it is however not confined to that (cf. *SC* 9). It is also mission, kerygma, didascalia, diakonia and a critical voice on political issues.

The achievement of the fifties

The achievement of this period is due mainly to A. G. Martimort. The famous liturgist Dom Guéranger with his guide through the year, *L'Année Liturgique*, had already set an approach to the Liturgy in terms of the voice of the Spouse very much along the lines that would be worked out theologically in *Mediator Dei*, but the educational media were slow to take it up. Liturgical theorising was, to start with, often concerned with rubrics. Then it became liturgical but concentrated mostly on studying various forms of cult with a tendency to give priority to ceremonial. Then it became theological but still with a touch of the rubrical about it. The liturgical movement which sought to present a truly living Liturgy nurtured,

111

and partly provoked, the renewal of the theology of the Church seen as the Body of Christ, and in its turn this absorbed the Liturgy. Thus *Mediator Dei* (1947) is based on *Mystici Corporis* (1943). In the work of some scholars (e.g., R. Guardini and P. Duployé) the anthropological and pastoral connotations really served to emphasise the ecclesial facet, whereas in point of fact the pastoral content might well have brought out the empirical and sociological slant. A. G. Martimort repeatedly approached the subject from an emphatically theological and even ecclesial angle. Thus, the liturgical assembly is not only *sacramentum*: it is the enactment of the Christian "mystery", an epiphany (manifestation) of the Church as Spouse and Body of Christ[1]. The Sunday assembly is an ecclesial organ of the Church and of Christian life[2]. The liturgical assembly is at one and the same time *sacramentum*[3], the Church rendered visible and functioning in conformity with the principles which determine the Church's structure, and *res sacramenti*, source of grace and unity in Christ[4].

Martimort was already taking his stand on issues which were later to be hotly debated, in particular with regard to principles that govern the structure of the Church: first, the traditional concept that the Church is made up of all and sundry and that it would be contrary to its ethos to try to create assemblies that are exclusive to one or another social or political set. Similarly the notion that the Church, and therefore the liturgical assembly, is of a kind that stands apart from any other organism as such. We shall come across these elements again in one form or another for they are met with nowadays more than ever before.

1. *La Maison-Dieu* 20 (1950).
2. *La Maison-Dieu* 40 (1954).
3. *La Maison-Dieu* 57 (1959).
4. *La Maison-Dieu* 60 (1959).

NEW FACTORS AND NEW PROBLEMS

Priority given to qualities of community

This arises as much from new problems as from new factors and in any case they are not all that new. But they have all come so much to the fore by way of opposition to the slant on cult as something purely social and precast and faceless that they now have to be taken into account as quite characteristic of present trends. This points to a very real need, a determination to have done with a merely superficial external relationship and to set up an interpersonal atmosphere instead, where people really know one another (on first name terms) and relate to one another, ready, so to speak, to rub shoulders. It carries a strong reaction against large assemblies geared to routine rituals. It involves something of a new way of seeing the Church or rather of what it means to live the life of the Church, implying basically that the Church must be in active harmony with the tangible realities of the community. We have already shown how our celebration of the Liturgy, whilst genuinely assuring mystical communion, failed to communicate a sense of a truly felt human community. You might say that the liturgical celebrations have been modelled on public gatherings where the people are simply an audience, and efforts have been made to remedy this by modifying church buildings and so on, creating a new style of celebration and all kinds of minute innovations.

Individual Churches

The notion that individual Churches do not stand apart from the universal Church as isolated entities is not all that new. As far back as 1937 we find the German scholar K. L. Schmidt, in an article on "Ekklesia" in Kittel's *Theologisches Wörterbuch*, asserting that each local Church is truly the Church of God in so far as this is present in such and such a place — the Church at Corinth, Paris, London, New York. . . . All the same, Rahner felt he could safely say that the most novel contribution Vatican II made to ecclesiology was the identification of the local Church with the one, holy, catholic and apostolic Church. The Council was mainly envisaging a diocese and gave a striking definition of it. "A diocese", it says, "is a section of the People of God entrusted to a bishop to be guided by him with the assistance of his clergy so that, loyal to its pastor and formed by him into one community in the Holy Spirit through the Gospel and the Eucharist, it constitutes one particular Church in which the one, holy, catholic and apostolic Church of Christ is truly present and active" (*Christus Dominus*, No. 11). Even at the level of the mystery of the Church as expressed in the Liturgy, the ideal thus presented is the one described by Ignatius of Antioch, namely, the Eucharistic assembly gathered round the bishop surrounded by his *presbyterium* (the priests of his diocese). But a priest, by the fact that he is sent to a place by his bishop, makes the bishop's presence a reality there. That is the point the Council is making in *Lumen Gentium* (No. 26): "This Church of Christ is really present in all legitimately organised local groups of the faithful which, in so far as they are united with their pastors, are also quite appropriately called Churches in the New Testament". Once again we meet the assertion that in the celebration of the Eucharist, which includes the proclamation of the Word of God, the Church makes itself fully and supremely a present reality.

This line of thought has been worked out by Father Nicolas Afanasieff under the heading of Eucharistic ecclesiology and was widely taken up by Orthodox theologians, though some of them queried it very much along the lines of criticisms levelled at it by Catholic theologians. The Eucharist is indeed the supreme means of occasion whereby the Church is made present in all its reality, but that does not mean that we overlook other factors such as the spoken word and unity of faith. On the other hand, given that the individual Churches are the local enactment of the universal Church, they are explicitly linked with that universality, which precisely as such has its own objective character and postulates a corresponding

114

structural pattern. They feed into that universality their own particular charisms and their own local history, and all this needs to be harmonised within a communion which is richer and more complex than each of the local Churches taken separately. These qualities belong to the fulness of the Church which has reserves far in excess of any given local Eucharistic Church. The Church is not only the Body of Christ but also the People of God.

This assessment of the individual Church or local Eucharistic community goes hand in hand with a renewal in the way of seeing the exact relationship between that community and the minister who presides at the celebration of the Eucharist. The theology of the sacrament of Holy Orders produced in the West between 1150 and 1250 presented the priest as personally qualified and dignified by a consecration which linked him with Christ and conferred on him a "power": *potestas conficiendi*, the power to "confect" the Eucharist. In the course of theological studies the tract on the sacraments was immediately followed by that on Christology and thus the study of the priest in the perspective of the community was bypassed. Nowadays he is presented in the context of *ecclesia* as the sacramentally ordained minister of a portion of the priestly laity. Priesthood is seen in the perspective of the community rather than directly and vertically in terms of Christ–priest. I once (writing in *Jalons*, 1953) found the expression "priesthood–laity" satisfactory. Today one would perhaps prefer "community–ministry". One is not altogether happy with the process that would express itself in terms of "from Christ to the priest, to the faithful". One would prefer: "from Christ to the Church with its ordained ministers". The community, just as much as the ministerial structure, has its origin in Christ's initiative and in his gift. Community and ministerial structure came into being together and neither has priority over the other. But they were brought into being with an established relationship between them by virtue of which the ministerial structure is the social expression, within the community, of that initiative and gift from Christ and is the sign that this comes from above and that the community is convoked by the Lord and does not just happen along together. One of the roles of the ordained priest is to guarantee the link with the explicit and tangible institution which goes back all the way to the Apostles and which, beginning in Jerusalem, has spread through the entire world.

Charisms and ministries

One of the greatest gains of the present day is the reinstatement of the notion of charisms and, linked with them, ministries (note the plural). The Church, especially as one experiences it in one's locality, is seen as the community which God builds up through the services which he brings into being and in view of which he makes the gift of vocations and abilities. Ministries differ from one another. Some are sacramental structures: they come from above although at the same time they belong very much within the community. Other recognised ministries are undoubtedly needed to ensure the smooth running of the community. But must we say, as Martimort does, that the lay people who exercise these latter ministries always need to be officially deputised. That is fairly obvious if by "always" you are thinking of the point at which a layperson takes up a ministry. But the term "officially deputised" seems to me to reflect a too clerical and juridical outlook which the Council and developments in Church life have now set aside. You do, of course, need some kind of recognition for every ministry that is to be exercised publicly in the Christian community. But if you use the word "deputised", does not that suggest that over and above making the exercise of the ministry legitimate you are granting the lay minister an entitlement which he or she already possesses by virtue of baptism and confirmation, charisms and the call of charity, as explained in *Apostolicam Actuositatem*, the decree on the apostolate?

In a later paragraph on the new things which have been introduced I shall place the permanent deacons. Their numbers vary from country to country. Maybe sometime

116

there will be women deacons too. As a matter of fact most of the kind of things assigned to deacons can be, and are already, done by lay men and women.

Church, sacrament of salvation

"Sacrament of salvation": a Church for the world. Of course the Church first and foremost exists for God and that is why precisely the Church seeks to win the world for God and take it to him in and through Jesus Christ. The theme of the Church as sacrament of salvation is one of the most fascinating aspects of the Council's treatment of ecclesiology. The Church is, by virtue of the redeeming Incarnation and Pentecost, the historical and public form given to the love of God for humankind manifested in the divine plan of grace and in the gift which he has made of his Son. The Church thus communicated his "mystery".

Nowadays particular interest is shown in what exactly is involved in this "salvation" of which the Church is the sign and the instrument. Does it mean only the forgiveness of sins? Does it not also take in humankind's liberation, not only from sin but also from all that degrades human beings socially? The answer surely is, Yes. The Church of course has its own ways and means of taking action and a particular level at which that action can be effectively taken, and neither is the same as those taken by specifically political movements. But on the other hand, being engaged in politics, in the best sense of that word, is part and parcel of the lives of many Christians today and therefore also a field in which their faith must find expression. And besides, the cult of the Christian community inevitably reflects and embraces the message of salvation in its widest possible meaning and is deeply concerned to foster it. So it is that the real meaning of "sacrament of salvation" will influence the form the Church's cult will take. Our liturgical celebration is thus brought into the field of the publicity and public image of the Church. And that involves its credibility also.

It has never been claimed that the Liturgy would exhaust the Church's field of action. The Church is called on today to be the instrument of the "loving kindness of God", to quote the Letter to Titus (3,4), in a world where people are being uprooted, left begging for help and a fair share for community, love and meaningful existence. Clearly, then, the Church can be neither the sign nor the instrument of salvation it is meant to be unless it acts both within and beyond the confines of its sacral framework and therefore beyond what happens in Church and in particular in the Eucharistic assemblies. There will then come into play all the work done by Caritas, Justice and Peace, help for the immigrants, education, leisure occupations. . . All of that can be related to the Church seen as sacrament of salvation, sign and instrument of the love and service of God for humankind. In this context there can be no doubt about Church meaning the People of God.

The idea of the Church as sign is uppermost in the minds of truly committed members of this People. A sign can be misleading or inadequately designed. There is nothing new about that. There are strong feelings today among those who reckon that the kind of signs the Church has devised for itself is inadequate. That does not mean that the criticisms are always well founded. The critics have sometimes not gone to the trouble of understanding what the signs are out to convey. But these reactions are not without their value. They often spring from a desire people have of working things out for themselves so that they are meaningful for *them*. People are more concerned with the question "does it work" than with "what does it mean in essence". Sometimes, it is true, asking "does it work" and "is it meaningful" leads to putting one's finger on what is of the essence of the matter in hand. But there is a danger of going for rules of interpretation on the spur of the moment and based purely on the human situation with which one happens to be faced and thus neglecting to take into account the criteria of Tradition. That kind of individualistic interpreting often lands one in insecurity. But such folks like the feeling of insecurity and often come pretty close to thinking it is a crime to use the prayer, found though it is in the Liturgy: "Grant peace to your Church in our times, O Lord".

118

Turning to the Eucharistic assembly itself, we find that its role as assembly and the aspects of fraternal repast, community feast and unity as fruit of the sacrament has all been brought to light with happy results. These are things which are associated with St Augustine's notions of *sacramentum* (visible achievement) and *res sacramenti* (the source of grace and unity). There is a danger today of neglecting the *res et sacramentum* of the Eucharist, the real presence of Christ sacrificed and glorified. It is true that a pure presence "in itself" (*in se*) creates a problem when it is a case of the presence of a living person and not of an object or an inanimate being. But we have before us the fact that Christ is substantially present in our Eucharist and in our communion.

Varied studies on the rites, feasts, etc.

There has been a real blossoming of studies on rites, symbols, gestures, festivity and physical attitudes. Some of them are related to ethnology, some to philosophy or psychology. We really are swamped with it. It must be admitted, however, that it has not made much practical impact on the Liturgy. The reason is that these studies are too theoretical and do not really get to grips with the actual celebration of the Liturgy. The Liturgy has its own distinctive traits and texture and leaves its own specific impression on those who take part in it. All said and done, however useful analysis and descriptions may be, we are immersed in the thought of the mystery of Christ in whom we believe, whom we love and in whom we live. Lastly, the new suggestions that are made are, once more, all too often sheer theory. There are some exceptions though. One does come across festive celebrations with a truly successful new look.

By and large, these liturgists indulge in rarified intellectualism. There is a lot of talking and explaining of one's views and many a simple gesture is high-handedly dismissed which expresses so well a wealth of confession of faith without recourse to finely defined concepts or even a spoken word. Take, for example the kissing of the altar

119

by the celebrant out of reverenece for it, or the sign of the cross made on forehead, lips and breast at the reading of the Gospel. We heard of a church where they decided not to use the Paschal Candle at the Easter Vigil. And yet it is such a wonderful and simple gesture with its steadily consuming flame and warmth, standing there as the risen Christ, a light and a sign of hope. But there are among the innovations some splendid gestures, full of meaning, like the human chain formed by the people holding hands during the Our Father.

An epoch open to discreet creativity

Many of the liturgical rules are meant to be a framework within which the on-going renewal and creation of new practices have to be fitted, as the Council's Constitution states (cf. *Sacrosanctum Concilium*, Nos 1, 21, 23, 62, 68). This proves to be quite productive as readers of *La Maison-Dieu* are aware. Normally the creation of new patterns should come out of the life of the genuine communities rather than out of studies done by specialists however useful these latter may be and even if they have taken the trouble to try out their new ideas before promoting them. The practical experience of the Christian community is in itself a source of theological thought which it is not easy to draw on for practical reasons. Yet it is a rich reserve of unsophisticated impact and life.

There is a delicate problem here regarding the relationship between innovations that emerge locally and the visual unity of the Church at large. There are quite a number of "experimental" liturgical prayers. The ancient usage is not against this in principle. The wording of the *anaphora* used to be left to the initiative of the celebrant. But one has to be sure that such prayers express the authentic faith of the Church. Experience shows that the problem here is very real. One reason however for allowing this kind of initiative is that it fosters "catholicity at horizontal level" and the acceptance within the framework of the universal Church of what the initiative

120

of a local Church has to offer. That presupposes that the local initiative is not a purely private venture but has already been found acceptable by the local Church and to be appropriate as an expression of the faith.

Small groups and their Eucharist

Some parishes are trying their best but are not getting anywhere. They never really get out into the open. The assembly is sometimes a mixture of people who are split over optional policies. The celebration fails to make use of what each member can contribute and is out of touch with real life. This criticism is in line with that levelled against everything that is institutionalised, predetermined without any regard for the people's choice. The community is numerically there all right, but the human factor is missing. No one really expresses their views, there is no joint effort in thinking things out, no exchange of ideas.

And yet an essential trait of an assembly is that it affords an opportunity for real gain amongst its members. That can be seen in some measure in those parishes that come under criticism the moment they get together. This needs thinking out. Just take the Letter to the Hebrews: "Let us hold fast the confession of our hope without wavering, for he who promised is faithful; and let us consider how to stir up one another to love and good works, not neglecting to meet together, as is the habit of some, but encouraging one another" (10,23–25). Compare this with 1 Peter 4,10. It is a known fact that being together, seeing one another at prayer, silently adoring together is a mutually comforting experience. This is true also of telling others about what God has put in our hearts and the understanding we have of his word. The Fathers often pointed this out and recommended it. It is what people have found in small groups who reflect together on the Gospel. They often prove to be Christian assemblies who feel the need to turn themselves into Eucharistic assemblies.

These latter must normally be presided over by a priest. The priest is truly a member of the community. In a sense he emerges from it. But he does not derive from it his role as president. That he owes to his ordination, which is derived by succession down the ages from the mission of Christ to the Apostles. Some people reject this and you will find a congregation where everybody says the Eucharistic Prayer including the words of Consecration. This is an error both theologically and liturgically, for if it is true that the whole assembly is supposed to take part in the entire celebration, it is wrong for all to claim to be entitled to do so in the self-same way. The celebration or liturgical assembly, like the Church itself, is regulated by a system of organisational law which provides for participation by all in the same activities but with different assigned roles. Ignoring this some people are heard to ask why one needs to be ordained to be able to celebrate the Eucharist, what is the specific role of the priest. Here and there (in some countries) one finds "Eucharistic" celebrations without an ordained priest. It is not easy to say exactly what they add up to. They can have a very real spiritual quality, dwelling as they do on Christ's death and his glorified life. But they are clean outside the Tradition of the Church, both Oriental and Western. They dismiss a coherent and weighty set of truths: the organisational character of the ecclesial body, the presentation of Christ in a clear relationship to the community which is not self-made nor self-convoked. And besides all this, there is the theology of Holy Orders as a sacrament which gives the grace (Oriental Church) and the power (Western Church) to celebrate the Sacred Mysteries.

Political solidarity and Eucharistic assembly

A good number of what are known as basic groups consist of people drawn together by a common political outlook. Pretty well everywhere Christians have become actively politically conscious and pledged to militance with movements for human liberation, protests on behalf of workers, undertakings for the creation of a better, more just, and brotherly society. There are practical consequences to the existence of tightly knit groups of this kind, such as treating others as social outcasts (cf. Jn 4,9).

1. Is it possible, some ask, for the exploiter and the exploited, the fulminator of oppression and his victim to participate and communicate in the same Eucharistic celebration?

2. In olden days the Church publicly sanctioned blatant injustices and sins that brought about serious social harm. The offerings of the rich who treated the poor harshly were refused, as were those people who lived in debauchery, traded dishonestly, bore false witness or were corrupt judges and so on. The oppression of the poor was punishable by excommunication. It is undoubtedly impossible to resuscitate these rules as such today. But how might one set about nowadays imparting a regard for the Christian mentality to which these practices gave expression? Has any effort been made to do so? Surely a truly genuine liturgical assembly demands it for the sake of its evangelical and Christian character.

3. How far is it necessary for a liturgical assembly to be a community at the human level in order to be authentic and achieve true communion? It would be too simplistic to count on an automatic transformation by virtue of the sacrament. We have already seen that the Eucharistic communion by itself does not produce a human sociological community. After all if it is true that the Eucharist produces the Church, it is the Church that brings the Eucharist. What meaning could there be in sharing only the Eucharist whilst remaining estranged with regard to every else of which our existence is composed? Writing about the youth J.-M. Domenach noted that young people find it intolerable that one should share in the Eucharist while not sharing in anything else. Clearly, this is a serious issue. It is a tangible reality. It is deeply felt. Our thoughts about it are linked with three propositions: the Eucharist by its very nature transcends unanimity; it implies, along with tolerating differences, a readiness for reconciliation; we need guidelines on the ethics of conflict.

1. A.-G. Martimort pointed out that the liturgical assembly is composed of all and sundry and gathers together sinners who acknowledge that that is what they are. Furthermore, say these writers, it occasions the breakdown in some measure of our human solidarity. One of the essential laws of the economy of salvation, it has been said, is that it gathers together people irrespective of their human factions. Dietrich Bonhoeffer, a reliable witness if ever there was one in this matter, wrote: "If we now ask ourselves where it is that faith affords the purest experience of being in the Church the answer is certainly not in communities made up of members who are all alike, united in a romantic feeling about solidarity, but rather where individuals are linked with one another by nothing except the ecclesial community, where Jew and Greek, pietist and liberal are thrown together and yet profess the self-same faith, praying for one another". That is a clear-enough statement, yet something needs to be added. For we can query what exactly the term "ecclesial community" comprises. Does it mean all those who frequent the church or a community of believers for whom profession of faith includes certain precise requirements regarding justice and fraternity? That brings us back to what we have said above. It remains true that the Eucharist is, of itself, a motive and a principle for being together which is absolutely original with regard to motives derived from unanimity on a purely human level. What united the faithful in the Eucharistic community in not only the call of Christ, faith in his Word, but his substantial presence which transcends all sociological, earthly and historical barriers and knits us together with at least the germ and call of eschatological reconciliation.

2. All this is in itself very real and very vast. But there is more besides. The people who meet in the assembly come just as they are, from different cultural environments, committed to different political conviction and to trade unions, all of which may turn out to be in opposition to each other. They may be people with

differing views on education or on burning issues like abortion, armed force, etc. Unless all this can be dismissed as superficial the people in the assembly will have to face up to these differences and take them for granted. But they must do so with an awareness that out and beyond these differences there is a focal point of reconciliation: Jesus Christ himself, who dominated and united them all. If we wanted to see this in terms of Bonhoeffer's categories we would place opposition in the second last and reconciliation in the last. But it is also true that the last renders the second last purely relative, without for all that stripping it of its real qualities. It does so not by denying the truths it contains but by adding its own reality to it. It follows that a unity devested of oppositions is eschatological. But a shared realisation of their eschatological destiny by peple who are in opposition to one another at the present time fosters in them a desire for reconciliation and communion.

That is precisely what the Eucharist presupposes. And this may call for formal acts of forgiveness and reconciliation. In Matthew 5,23–24 we read: "If you are offering your gift at the altar, and there remember that your brother has something against you, leave your gift there before the altar and go; first be reconciled with your brother, and then come and offer your gift". It may well be, however, that one has to bide one's time before this reconciliation can take place and it may even prove to be impossible to achieve it. What one is in duty bound to do is to take full advantage of what possibilities there are. And at the same time, we must not set our sights too low!

3. There is a certain way of conceiving unity, communion and reconciliation that fails to realise that conflict can be quite earnest and legitimate. There is a whole set of Catholic morals that presumes that conflicts are always sinful. It looks on human passions in the same way. This cast of mind is associated with a childish type of hagiography and iconography. We need a picture of unity that comprises conflicts and pluralism and a system of ethics to go with it.

This opens up a field of investigation too vast to be dealt with here. We shall leave aside the complex question of secularisation as such and even an exhaustive treatment of what one calls the secularisation of the Liturgy. The drift of the latter is that it wants to bring the Liturgy in line with the changes that have taken place in present-day culture instead of keeping it in a separate cultural setting derived from our Catholic past. This change involves a readiness to adopt the kind of language people use in everyday life and a distrust regarding statements about the supernatural that are rooted in our historical past but which have not kept pace with history and this at a time when there is a lack of awareness of God. Lastly, it objects to segregated action since Christ has sanctified all things in his own person and eliminated the distinction between the sacred and the profane world. This trend has given rise to a variety of statements ranging from questionable and dangerous reductionist formulas to others fundamentally legitimate and sound: "It is becoming increasingly clear that Christianity is not being integrated even amongst Christians, in the totality of human life. Its way of thinking and its Liturgy constitute a world apart, isolated, an aside world halted in an outdated ontology, a sacramental concept with no grip on real life or the world of action". It is quite possible that, even within such limits as that, the problem may include the more radical types we have mentioned. There is no denying the existence of the problem and it has a direct bearing on the liturgical assembly. The problem is how to bring into play all that the liturgical celebration stands for and contains.

All the faithful individually make personal spiritual sacrifices, acting in this as their own priest, and thus offering their daily life with its own setting and background. But the sacramental Liturgy must not be thought of as a mere prolongation or sum total of these sacrifices. The Eucharist, the sacraments, are something quite different; they are the acts of Christ, our Saviour,

our Mediator, our Lord. The personal sacrifices must be integrated into this, Christ's sacrifice, for the mystery of Christ is brought about in his Body the Church, whereas the spiritual sacrifices made by Christians reach the Father only in Christ and united with the Pasch of Christ. The problem is how to bridge the gulf between the work-a-day week and Sunday worship. That is brought about largely through preaching and the universal Prayer. The choice of language and the use of the right kind of gestures also come into it. Ought not the faithful to take a more active part? That is almost impossible in the normal large assemblies. It can perhaps be done in assemblies for special festivals well prepared in advance and looked on as a bit exceptional, life Y.C.W. Congresses. "Paraliturgy" is the term likely to be used for that kind of event, though need the "para" really be added? It must also be admitted that it is difficult to make a success of such celebrations if the everyday, "secular" elements to be woven in are largely of a political cast. But if that is what the people's life is really like, how can we close the doors on it? There must be some means of bringing the Gospel right into the environment without it ceasing to be truly the Gospel of Jesus Christ.

We have not overlooked the fact that all these matters we have been looking at have their bearing on the kind of building a place of worship should be. You can find cases where the adaptation has been overdone, real exhibitions of banality. There is no need for that, though admittedly this adaptation is no easy task. We cannot go into it here apart from saying that the requirements of good taste and code of behaviour and the options foreseen by ecclesiology need to be taken into account. Is the Church, one needs to ask, only to be seen as a portion .of the world that confesses Christ? It is certainly that, but is it not surely something more? Has not its distinctive visual presentation likewise special requirements in this matter?

We bring this paragraph to a close with a general observation that may throw light on certain current facts. We are today witnessing a movement which is the reverse of what was going on right through 1500 years and especially during the Middle Ages. The practice then was to stress the differences and to segregate specific settings from the common run of things, making of them something quite special and standing apart, thus, for instance, the pope with regard to the bishops and the Church at large, the priest with regard to the people, religious with regard to the laity, the sacraments with regard to the general sacramentality of the Church, the Virgin Mary with regard to the Church, the saints and their miracles as distinct from ordinary Christian life, the liturgical ceremonies as distinct from life in general and global culture. Today we are witnessing the opposite process which may also have its excesses and its one-sided approach: it would be easy to list examples of them. But the key to sound judgement in all this must be sought in a synthesis and integration.

Liturgical assemblies and ecumenical requests

Ecumenism has brought new kinds of Christian assemblies into existence. It would be difficult to refuse to describe some of them as "liturgical". We are not thinking here of outlandish celebrations. There are some kinds of celebration which are canonically approved of, though the form they take is not always satisfactory. In the matter of Eucharistic celebrations we come up against a fundamental issue, namely, that sharing a Eucharistic celebration means belonging to the same Church. Here we must once more denounce a kind of Eucharistic inflation, however profound the sentiments may be of those who go so far as to share the Eucharist with non-Catholics. But apart from the Eucharist there are forms of praying together, sharing the Word of God, and "charismatic" (a questionable term here) types of meetings. And there are other occasions of communal celebration such as mixed marriages which one finds in some places rather movingly described as ecumenical marriages. Thanks to fervent mixed families there is beginning to be a tendency to make a sort of ecumenical Church which, on the basis of the double religious affinity in these families, would emerge

128

into a third entity. Some people are talking about "ecumenical Baptism" by virtue of which one would become a Christian without being exclusively Catholic or Protestant. But is it really possible to have an ecclesial no man's land? Is Karl Barth's statement no longer valid? He said that you cannot be in the *una sancta invisibilis* (the invisible one holy Church) unless you belong to the *una sancta visibilis*, that is to say, to one or another part of the divided Church. Or must we see a new sign of the times in ecumenism which, because it is a "movement", cannot be fitted into homologous categories?

Chapter 11

Liturgical celebration and witness*

Liturgical language

The Liturgy is a spoken witness to faith. Independently of the homily, the Liturgy is vocal from beginning to end.

The texts. The witness given by the spoken word mainly takes the form of narratives telling what God has done and what he is actually doing. The reading from the Gospels are such narrative. It is the practice today to reflect on that particular aspect of witness which a narrative provides with the special kind of impact it makes. The story of great events has always played a role in civic and national history. The same holds good from the Christian angle.

Gestures. Alongside the texts we have the liturgical gestures which are so often full of meaning. Their importance as witness and as a medium for teaching the faith should be stressed. Many of them which had their origin in monastic tradition have unfortunately disappeared. Simple and beautiful that they are, the gestures have a style of their own and as symbols are highly instructive, thus for instance the fact of taking off one's hat on entering a church, of making the sign of the cross, genuflecting, kneeling down, or bowing out of reverence for the cross in the Good Friday Liturgy. A gesture or a symbol can be much more telling than the best-worded phrase. Love, for instance, expressed by kissing, and without a single word spoken, expresses far more than anything said could convey. In the same way a simple sign of the cross, even if it is done without all that much concentration, enshrines all the content of a treatise

* *Cahiers St Dominique* (June 1976).

on the Redemption and on the Holy Trinity. And it is truly an open profession of faith in the Holy Trinity and the Redemption.

In the Eucharistic celebration, by repeating the words of Jesus, "Do this in memory of me", one is not only proclaiming but actually doing. And St Paul tells us: "As often as you *do* this you proclaim the Lord's death until he comes" (cf. 1 Cor 11,26).

Thus in what is done in the liturgical celebration there is a wealth of expression and instruction.

Doxologies. The word "doxology" comes from the Greek, meaning "spoken praise". In the Liturgy a considerable amount of instruction is given through praise addressed to God. Thus the "Glory be to the Father, and to the Son, and to the Holy Spirit", which is a particularly meaningful doxology, sums up in a proclamation of praise the whole dogmatic substance of the Holy Trinity. There is actually no explicit statement in the New Testament about the divinity of the Holy Spirit, a fact that gave rise to many a theological discussion in the fourth century. But on the other hand there are many texts about the Trinity, something like forty of them, more than thirty in St Paul. For instance, take the one we now say at the beginning of Mass which is the last verse of the Second Letter to the Corinthians: "The grace of our Lord Jesus Christ and the love of God and the fellowship of the Holy Spirit be with you all". The assembly makes this its own by replying, "Amen", which creates the liturgical atmosphere in which priest and people are linked together.

But how did a theology of the Trinity grow out of these formulas? St Basil, Bishop of Caesarea, used the formula "Glory be to the Father with the Son and with the Holy Spirit" in which, therefore, the glory given to the Son was assimilated to that given to the Father and the glory given to the Holy Spirit assimilated to that given to both one and the other. This brought criticism from some of the people in the liturgical assembly because they had never heard that kind of formula used before. Basil replied to the criticism in his treaty on the Holy Spirit, written about A.D. 375. In it he justified the formula on the grounds of the order given by

Jesus to "go and baptise all nations in the name of the Father, and of the Son, and of the Holy Spirit". "Our praise", wrote Basil, "must echo our belief and we must believe that with which we were baptised". Later on, that same doxology was taken up in the Nicaean Creed drawn up at the Council of Constantinople in 381. Basil's formula thus found its way into the *Credo* of the Mass: "*Qui cum Patre et Filio simul adoratur*" ("with the Father and the Son he is worshipped and glorified"). Without saying explicitly that the Holy Spirit is God, he is paid the same glory and worship.

In this way, then, the Liturgy is full of dogmatic statements about God.

We may give some more examples of the doctrinal content of doxologies in the New Testament. They are so compact that they would need easily fifteen to twenty lectures from an expert to analyse them fully.

There is, for instance, the beginning of the Letter to the Romans. It reads: "Paul, a servant of Jesus Christ, called to be an apostle, set apart for the gospel of God which he promised beforehand through his prophets in the holy Scriptures, the gospel concerning his Son, who was descended from David according to the flesh and designated Son of God in power according to the Spirit of holiness by his resurrection from the dead, Jesus Christ our Lord, through whom we have received grace and apostleship" (1,1–5).

Then there is the great hymn in the Letter to the Philippians which may well be a hymn used by the first Christians dating from before St Paul wrote and therefore also before the Gospels were written: "Jesus Christ, who, though he was in the form of God, did not count equality with God a thing to be grasped, but emptied himself, taking the form of a servant, being born in the likeness of men. And being found in human form he humbled himself and became obedient unto death, even death on a cross. Therefore God has highly exalted him and bestowed on him the name which is above every name, that at the name of Jesus every knee should bow, in heaven and on earth and under the earth, and every tongue confess that Jesus Christ is Lord, to the glory of God the Father" (2,6–11).

The spoken word of the Liturgy, then, has a distinctive style and these doxologies, full as they are of dogmatic assertions, make use of a declamatory language that enlists a response from the listener. Many of the liturgical texts, especially in the celebration of the sacraments, use this style proclaiming something that is being done to the persons addressed and eliciting a sense of reception on their part. For example, "I baptise you in the name of the Father, and of the Son, and of the Holy Spirit", or, "I absolve you from your sins".

The actors in the Liturgy

In the celebration of the Liturgy we exercise our baptismal priesthood in keeping with the First Letter of Peter: "Like living stones be yourselves built into a spiritual house, to be a holy priesthood, to offer spiritual sacrifices acceptable to God through Jesus Christ . . . you are a chosen race, a royal priesthood, a holy nation, God's own people, that you may declare the wonderful deeds of him who called you out of darkness into his marvellous light" (2,5.9).

This text, so full of profound thought and exhuberant joy, is enormously dynamic: living stones, inserted in the structure of the temple; we are ourselves individually and collectively a temple. Every single soul is rightly called a temple and so is the Church. "To offer spiritual sacrifices", that is, to offer spiritually the sacrifice of our life, not in a sort of moral masochism, but in sheer joy. We bring to life our Godwardness made "acceptable to God through Jesus Christ". Further on Peter points out that witness also comes into play in this setting. It finds expression in several ways — proclamation, communication, teaching, the spoken word, upbringing, writing and, of course, celebration. We proclaim the praises of him who called us "out of darkness into his marvellous light".

In the celebration, then, we are there as priests by virtue of our baptism, rendering glory to God and hallowing his name.

It is interesting to note that in the Ecumenical Translation of the Bible instead of "hallowed be thy name" (Mt 6,9) we read: "Make yourself known as God". Rightly or wrongly the translators reckoned that the phrase "hallowed be", expressive though it undoubtedly is for Jews, is less so for the modern reader. What is offered is not exactly a translation but a good way of putting it. That can be far reaching. For if we celebrate God, if we declare his name holy, we are proclaiming him God and, so to speak, bring into play his Godhead.

That is what Rabbi Simeon Ben Yohai had in mind when, writing in A.D. 150, he makes God say: "If you are my witnesses, I am your God". That is very close to what Isaiah says: "'You are my witnesses', says the Lord, 'and my servant whom I have chosen, that you may know and believe me and understand that I am He. Before me no God was formed, nor shall there be any after me. I, I am the Lord, and besides me there is no saviour. I declared and saved and proclaimed, when there was no strange god among you; you are my witnesses', says the Lord" (43,10–12).

"You are my witnesses and I, I am your God", says Isaiah. In writing, "If you are my witnesses, I am your God", the Rabbi has pointed out the connection between the two statements. Of course, God is God even if no one bears witness to him but then he is not acknowledged as God. He is only acknowledged in so far as we bear witness to him. That is one of the purposes of liturgical celebration. It is we who function in that celebration, comprising the Christian community and its presiding minister ordained for that purpose, the animator of the assembly, holding it together as a unit and giving expression to its faith and speaking in its name.

Witness in the presence of others

Who are these "others"? First of all they are all the members of the faithful present at the celebration, a community comprising nowadays a certain number of lukewarm folk, half-hearted believers and people who only attend from time to time. On the special family occasions like marriage, baptisms and especially funerals, many people come out of sympathy or friendship, even if they do not share our faith. It is in such circumstances that the witness of the Liturgy can play an important role; and there are many instances when, especially, once more, at funerals, if the style of the celebration is beautifully worked out and the celebrant has said a few well-chosen words, these people have been swept off their feet and are heard to say afterwards that they never dreamt it was like that.

In the Liturgy we do indeed witness to the Sacred Mysteries and that witness besides being directed to the glory of God and for our benefit is also quite a revelation to others, strengthening the faith of the lukewarm and the half-hearted believers and may be stirring up the consciences of those who "just happen" to be there.

The same kind of effect can be produced by our sacred buildings. Napoleon, on visiting Chartres Cathedral, said that an atheist would be ill-at-ease there. A great many conversions are due to visits of that kind. There was once a sacristan who used to show people round and explain the carvings and the stained-glass windows and on every occasion it had its effect on one or another of the visitors.

Another instance of the effect of being present at a liturgical celebration is the case of the famous English sculptor Eric Gill. While still a non-believer he visited the monastery of Mont César in Louvain which at the time was a centre of the liturgical movement. Eric Gill described how he watched the unhurried procession of the monks coming into the church and how they knelt for a few moments in silence and then suddenly stood and intoned the *"Deus in adiutorium meum intende"*. It was the first time he had ever witnessed it or heard that invocation and he said he knew with absolute certainty from that moment that God existed and that he was a living God.

There can be no doubt that this role of the Liturgy as a medium for making known the Sacred Mysteries — hierophany, as this effect is called — is very real. A passage from Malcolm Muggeridge's book on Mother Teresa of Calcutta[1] gives a further instance of it. Muggeridge was sent by the British Broadcasting Corporation to do a television programme about her and her work for the destitute and the dying in India, now so well known. He wrote:

> The verdict on the Mother Teresa interview was that, technically, it was barely usable, and there was for a while some doubt whether it was good enough for showing at all except late at night. In the end it was put out on a Sunday evening. The response was greater than I have known to any comparable programme, both in mail and in contributions of money for Mother Teresa's work. I myself received many letters enclosing cheques and money-orders ranging between a few shillings and hundreds of pounds. They came from young and old, rich and poor, educated and uneducated; all sorts and conditions of people. All of them said approximately the same thing – this woman spoke to me as no one ever has, and I feel I must help her.
>
> Discussions are endlessly taking place about how to use a mass medium like television for Christian purposes, and all manner of devices are tried, from dialogues with learned atheists and humanists to pop versions of the psalms and psychedelic romps. Here was the answer. Just get on the screen a face shining and overflowing with Christian love; someone for whom the world is nothing and the service of Christ everything; someone reborn out of servitude to the ego and flesh and into the glorious liberty of the children of God. Then it doesn't matter how the face is lighted or shot: whether in front or profile, close-up or two-shot or long-shot; what questions are put, or by whom. The message comes over, as it did from St Paul – not, it would appear, particularly glib or photogenic himself. It might seem surprising, on the face of it, that an obscure nun of Albanian origins, very nervous – as was clearly apparent – in front of the camera, somewhat halting in speech, should reach English viewers on a Sunday evening as no professional Christian apologist, bishop or archbishop, moderator or knockabout progressive

---

1. M. Muggeridge, *Something Beautiful for God* (Collins/Fount).

dog-collared demonstrator ever has. But this is exactly what happened, to the surprise of all professionally concerned, including me. The message was the same message that was heard in the world for the first time two thousand years ago; as Mother Teresa showed, it has not changed its sense or lost its magic. As then, so now, it is brought, "not with enticing words of man's wisdom, but in demonstration of the Spirit and of power; that your faith should not stand in the wisdom of men, but in the power of God" (1 Cor 2,4–5).

That is what hierophany is; God revealed through what someone says, by the expression on their face, their bearing and personality.

How often our liturgical celebrations achieve that is an open question. It does sometimes happen; for instance, at the Mass celebrated by so-and-so or at a particular function. But at other times nothing occurs despite the fact that one has done and said everything one ought to. We cannot expect to reveal God in this way every time. But we can always have it in view, for a liturgical celebration has the inherent quality of witness.

It also has an immense educational quality, education, that is, in its fullest meaning, which is not limited to instruction. If we look back and ask ourselves what really influenced us in our childhood, we shall find that we owe what we are much less to what we learnt in class or talks we listened to than to the sense of values we derived from the milieu in which we lived.

This idea is very well explained in a passage in a book entitled *The Saint, the Genius and the Hero* by the German philosopher Max Scheler. It runs:

The second means by which example exercises an effective influence is what we call tradition. It fits in between what is conveyed by heredity and the modality of reception, instruction and upbringing in the process of comprehension. It makes an automatic and vital impact. It consists in absorbing certain types of thinking, choosing and assessing things, simply thanks to the fact that our milieu rubs off on us and we mechanically imitate it. In a word, under the influence of tradition we do not even realise that an impact is

137

being made on us. The will of another does duty for our own. We do not weigh matters up before adopting them, we do not make a choice. We have the impression that what is transmitted to us is the outcome of our own perception and assessment. Children unconsciously absorb from their close surroundings a way of thinking, a set of values, a way of behaving and of speaking and a type of mannerisms, all acquired because it is part and parcel of the life they were living long before they were able to understand what it all meant. And thanks to this influence the main traits of what the child will be later on in life have already begun to take shape in him or her.

We can see this same process at work in the role the Liturgy has played in our upbringing in the faith. We are thinking of course of those of us who have attended the Liturgy regularly and not just occasionally. It has moulded in us, without our noticing it, a Christian, Catholic soul.

Chapter 12

Heaven, the world's burning bush*

In France in July 1968 Catholic and Protestant broadcasts
made comments on the recent major social and political
disturbances. This brought a rebuke from the spokesman
for the television authorities who told the directors of
religious programmes: "If you are allowed time on
television it is in order to enable you to broadcast the Mass
and to talk about heaven and not about what goes on here
on earth!"[1]

Heaven is what I want to talk about in this chapter. In
some ways that is all too easy but in other ways very
difficult indeed. It is all too easy if all you do is talk about
it in the purely imaginary and conventional fashion, using
the highly coloured and gilded dreams so vacuous that
they leave you on the fringe of unreality. It is a picture of
asexual beings, weightless, perched on clouds and singing
"Alleluia". Someone said: "Heaven is tasteless; hell is
spiced. I prefer hell". So much the worse for him! But it
does set us thinking. We cannot be content with that
childish imagery. Let us hope people will be able to pick
out the facts from it and see them in all their reality,
worthy of God, of ourselves and of the world.

Heaven has a relationship to the realities of our present
life. It is our final end and the fulfilment of our desires,
but it brings our aspirations to a fulfilment out and

---

*   *La Vie Spirituelle* (January 1977).
1. *Le Monde* (19 July 1968). Similar admonitions by M. Sanguinette, member
of UDR for Haute-Garonne, *Le Monde* (22 June 1971) and Admiral de Joybert
to the bishops: "Your work, my Lord Bishops, is to teach the faith and foster
charity. On the face of it, that is a hard enough task. Restrict your activities to
that, for God, and leave the State, which has due respect for the spiritual sphere,
to look after what are its tasks" (*Le Figaro*, 14–15 July 1973).

beyond their own reach and anything we can at present picture to ourselves. That assertion is based on two truths found in the Bible, the Word of God: this world is still unfulfilled; to know the true nature of anything you must grasp the end for which it exists and that is only discovered in God who called it into existence.

Christian teaching has rightly been focussed on the events of Easter, the resurrection of Christ crucified and buried. Significantly, too, the Liturgy makes us begin Lent, which is the beginning of our "going up to Jerusalem", by reading the account of the creation in Genesis and has us read it again during the solemn Easter Vigil. The point is that the "second" creation, the new and final one, presupposes the first. Our hope is rooted in faith. It is faith that shows us that we and the world depend on "God the Father almighty, maker of heaven and earth", as we declare at the beginning of the Creed. The God of our faith is already there as the unseen origin and cause of our present existence. He who is also the God of our hope will be, in a new way and this time for all to see, the cause and principle of a new and radiant kind of existence after his perfect likeness.

In this perspective the present world is seen as the first and only partly completed phase of an undertaking which postulates a second phase. This is an extremely important point when you come to reflect about the enormous problem of evil, but equally so when you try to grasp what it means to believe in heaven and hope to attain it. What does transpire is that if the "beyond" does exist it is a "beyond" that is not something foreign to this present life. There is to be a re-start so to speak, purified of all evil. The Scriptures speak of a "new heaven and a new earth in which righteousness dwells" (2 Pet 3,13). We shall see presently how this heaven exists here on earth and the continuity it ensures with our present life.

Between the beginning and the end

The condition of life in this present world has been ably described by some great thinkers and we shall draw on what they had to say in our reflections here. Kant has shown that our scientific and confirmed knowledge is subject to the conditions of space and time. But they are conditions that make for separateness and isolation. Anything that lies at a distance from me, however limited that may be, is not present to me. Even our neighbours can be strangers to us. And it does not demand a great length of time for things to cease to be present. I forget so easily and I rarely foresee. Precious little of the reality of this world comes objectively into my little orbit of life. People and things are exterior to us, even foreign and adverse towards us. We suffer from this distancing because we are made for love from others and towards others, for harmony, unity, peace, and communal life. But, as it is, things are impenetrable and often wound and overpower us. People, too, are often impenetrable for us and fence themselves in, jealous of their privacy. We are all constantly rebuffed by one another's secretiveness. Each of us is his or her own prisoner. Sartre declares, in his book *Huisclos*: "Frank openness should surely come to take the place of secrecy. I picture to myself the day when two people will have no secrets from each other quite simply because they will keep no secrets from anybody and the personal will be as freely shared as the air we breathe". And in reply to the question, what are the main obstacles to this universal openness, Sartre replied: "The foremost obstacle is the existence of what I call the Ill. By that I mean that actions are inspired by different sets of principles and can end up with results of which one disapproves. This Ill makes communication of ideas constantly difficult because one does not know how far the other person's principles which shape his thinking tally with one's own".

That is a theory of a philosopher drawn up by him within his own pattern of thought. In its own particular fashion it strikes a note with the experience and the teaching of sound spiritual Christians. Another saying of Sartre, "hell is other folk", finds a ready answer from Christian thinking: hell is a place where God is not to be found, the place of radical absence, where there is nothing that can unite people with one another. Spiritual writers have often spoken of this situation of opposition and conflict, disorder and confusion which is ours. They have sometimes called it *"regio dissimilitudinis"*, a universe of dissimilitude, of anti-openness and non-communication.

Origen has an interesting and enlightening notion, namely, that we do not get to grips with or take account of either the origins of reality or its ultimate end which are concealed from us, but only with the milieu of reality. And yet man cannot avoid asking questions about it all. Where do we come from? Where and to what are we going? Religions offer answers; it is their business to do so. Myths offer answers, too. They come up with the poetical replies about what there was beforehand and how it all worked out. They have little enough to say what came after. But everyday life goes on regardless of these burning questions. And so does science and leisure and social life and politics. For they are all totally immersed in the limitations of this present world, that is, in the milieu of the real, between its origin and its end. The sense of the purpose and finality of things and of life is likewise replaced by a sense of what is within things and life in themselves, in their internal limitations which isolate them and set up oppositions among them. In biblical terms it means being abandoned to the world of appearances and not of reality, to a void and not the fulness of being. Thus in Romans: "For creation was subjected to futility, not of its own will but by the will of him who subjected it to hope" (8,20).

God all in all

Indeed the source and origin of all is the divine generosity desiring to communicate itself and, so to speak, exist outside of itself. The end in view is the success and consummation of this enterprise. It can be called salvation if we recall the militant, perilous and onerous conditions that go with it. St Paul sums it up completely in few words which are one of the boldest and most profound pronouncements of the whole of Revelation: "God will be everything to everyone" (RSV Bible) or "all in all" (other versions) (1 Cor 15,28). There you have his kingdom, and heaven is exactly that. After all, heaven, on our side, is a certain state of being, blossoming with life; on God's side, it is nothing other than his presence, his glory, the full radiance of his benevolence. It is God himself shining like the ideal Sun, it is the finite totally penetrated and irradiated by the infinite. We shall be told: "Enter into the joy of your Master" (Mt 25,21). We spontaneously picture heaven as the symbol of transcendence: what we speak of as "on high" is thus naturally thought of as an attribute of the divinity. John Robinson set out to demythologise our spacial religious imagery and suggested replacing "on high" with "inside" (which just happens to be spacial as well!)[2]. The reality is something more profound and integral: the "on high" becomes "within". Heaven, which is God in his transcendence, is wholly immanent, "God all in all". "The first man, Adam, became a living being (one receiving life); the last Adam became a life-giving spirit" (1 Cor 15,45). In the creation in which we are here on earth, in order to keep alive we have to take in things from outside of ourselves, and that means taking, even killing and destroying. We get our knowledge from things and, by the same token, we are subservient to them. In order to keep alive we snatch away plants and animals; and that means that we are destroying life. That is the logical pattern in which the life of the first Adam is enclosed. We even look on other human beings in terms of our own requirements. Like vipers we suck the blood of other beings. That is the logical pattern of the "flesh". But the pattern of the spirit is quite the reverse. It does not take life; it gives it, radiates it. This supposes a transformation by God's work within us. St Augustine never tires of reflecting on it and preaching about it. He says: "We shall be filled to overflowing by our God. He in himself will be the replacement of anything and everything we could set our hearts on here on earth. There is, for instance, our appreciation and desire of food and

2. J. Robinson, *Honest to God*.

our search for it: God will be our nourishment; there is the desire for human embrace: "but for me it is good to be near God" (Ps 71,28); here on earth you are out to acquire a wealth: how could any single thing be lacking to you when you possess the One who has created all things? And the Apostle Paul himself gives us his word for it in speaking of that life we have just been describing when he says: "So that God may be all in all" (1 Cor 15,28). We shall all have the shared vision and common possession of God and he will be our common peace. He himself will replace in himself all the good things he gives us now.

The fact that freedom consists in not being under pressure from outside but in making up our own minds from within will help us to catch a glimpse of what St Paul means when, having recalled our state of slavery and futility in this world, he speaks about the hope of being freed from bondage and obtaining the "glorious liberty of the children of God" (Rom 8,21). The personal state which enables us to act from within ourselves (interiority), if it is totally unhindered (absolute), ensures absolute freedom. The absolute interiority of God brings the absolute freedom of the children of God. That freedom is "glorious", for the glory of God is his radiant presence shining in us and radiating out of us. Incidentally, that is what the halo on statues and pictures of the saints is trying to tell us. That light, or flame, is God present in us as the source of all life, all knowledge, all love and all joy. In this connection St Maximus the Confessor recalls the burning bush (cf. Ex 3,2) which burnt without being consumed. Moses turned aside to look at this object which was all aglow but did not burn itself out, and it was God who called him to him out of the bush and revealed his name to him: "I am who I am". In other words, I am the one who imparts being. He gives us our being at present for a perishable life. He, the self-same, will hereafter give us being for absolute, imperishable life. Hans Urs von Balthasar works this out, with ample reference to Maximus' writings, thus: "Just as the soul is present in every part of the body, so shall God be present in the world. . . The present world in which we live will be transformed within God, its total being entering into the total being of God, its unity meeting the Unity, the splendour of God enveloping it like the sun outshining the stars, all its parts made subservient to the reign that rules over everything. All self-will ceases to be because the creature no longer wishes to belong to itself. There is now only one activity, the activity of God himself and thus there is supreme freedom. The symbol of the burning bush thus comes fully into its own. The ineffable and prodigious fire hidden in the very essence of things as in the burning bush will revere itself, but not in order to consume the world, for it needs no fuel to stay alight. It will be a fire of love deep within all things and that fire will be God"[3].

Existing for the sake of others

This would be the place, if space permitted, to work out a theology of thanksgiving, that superb and delicate state of soul which bridges any gap there may be between what we receive and what we give. Heaven itself will be thanksgiving. However, what we must do here is to return to the very core of our present subject and show that this Presence is the source and principle of total communion. God, indeed, is all in *all*, the flame of light and love that burns in each of us without ever burning us up, that is, without destroying each one's distinctive personality. And since it is the same in each and everyone it constitutes then source and principle of an infinitely profound communion. We call it the Communion of Saints. Here on earth we only live in that Communion by faith, and, indeed, in a way that remains a mystery, and so we speak of the "Mystical Body". But when we come into the "glory" of heaven it will be opened up and be completely transparent and luminous, thanks to beatific charity, the same charity which we know on earth, "for love never ends" (1 Cor 13,8), but unfolded into full light because from then on its source and principle presents itself as

3. H. Urs von Balthasar, *Liturgie cosmique: Maxime le Confesseur*, Théologie II (Paris 1947).

totally luminous and supremely radiant. When Sartre, whom we quoted above, was speaking about transparence, he said it could be impeded if different people acted from different motives and on different principles. Philosophers speak of "reciprocity of consciences". That is exactly the case: a self-same transparence, communication, existence, shared with and for one another.

In the New Testament heaven, or the kingdom of God, is presented as a unanimous, joyful assembly: a banquet (Mt 8,11; Lk 13,29 and 14,15), a marriage feast (Mt 22,2; 7,13–17; 14,1–5), a firmly set city, Jerusalem (Heb 12,22; Rev 21,10 and 22,15). And Thomas Aquinas, in a commentary on *"vitam aeternam"* in the Creed, said: "Eternal life consists in the joyful society of all the Blessed. What makes this society a supremely delightful one is the fact that each and every one of its members will share equally all they have. Each loves all the others as he loves himself and is as happy about another's well-being as if it were his own. And so the greater the happiness of any one member the greater the happiness of all".

In the Spirit and in fire

"Love never ends". Here on earth, it is true, it does not enjoy the beatific transparence and absolute self-giving that knows no limitation of space and time, but its nature as a principle of communion is already in evidence and it is already rooted in the Holy Spirit. "God's love has been poured out into our hearts through the Holy Spirit who has been given to us" (Rom 5,5). Both the *Ecumenical Bible* and the *Jerusalem Bible* point out that this text is speaking of the love which is God's own and with which he loves us. Thus we are already endowed with the very principle on which heaven rests. We are already that new creation which must renew this world in which we are now living and bring it to fulfilment (cf. Gal 6,15; 2 Cor 5,17; Rom 6,4 and 7,6). But that life is "hid with Christ in God. When Christ our life appears, then you also will appear with him in glory" (Col 3,3; Eph 2,19; 1 Jn 3,1–2). We are still living here on earth in the flesh (cf. 2 Cor 10,3) but, in and through Christ, we live the life of the children of God.

To take up the categories set out by Origen, we can rightly say that the origin and end, which correspond to each other, are present in the milieu in which our present life is spent. But they are hidden. Only those who know and love God are aware of them and they here and now give thanks to God. These people are the priests of the creation, the interpreters of the sighs with which, as the Scriptures say, creation awaits the revelation of God.

Perfect communion which overcomes the divisions of space and time is, like its source, the Holy Spirit, an eschatological reality. But like the Holy Spirit that communion is given as an earnest. Its perfect bond is charity, love (cf. Col 3,14). Love brings others into my life. It makes them present to me despite the distance that may separate them from me. Love even now bridges the gaps made by space and time and, indeed, unites all those whom Christ has reconciled "whether on earth or in heaven" (Col 1,20). It is, in truth, because of Christ and through the Holy Spirit that that which will be achieved perfectly and in full light in heaven has already its beginning here on earth, in the Mystical Body. Because "in Christ the whole fulness of deity dwells" (Col 2,9), he can be all in all and bring about that God is here and now "through all and in all" (Eph 4,6). Out and beyond what we ourselves can see, which is in the sphere of history and geography (space and time), the catholicity of the Body of Christ remains a mystery: "I believe in the catholic Church". The great Scholastics, in commenting on these words of the Creed, linked with them the article on the Holy Spirit: I believe in the Holy Spirit who makes the Church one, holy, catholic and apostolic. How the juridical and sociological angles on the Church seem inadequate in the face of this spiritual reality! Nevertheless the provision of genuine community facilities does foster the spiritual ideal of communion at the level of the physical reality of our life in this world.

The world of tangible things is our assigned setting in which we live out our lives, and within it we are in advance in a limited degree, something of a fulfilment of the end for which it has all been created. In this way there exists a continuity between the "here below" and "the world to come". They are not two spheres of existence totally cut off from each other. The phrase "heaven and earth" can serve to indicate two states of one and the same human life while at the same time pointing to the light that one throws on the other, namely, on the one hand the temporal condition of human beings during their earthly existence and on the other hand their condition in eternity[4].

We have been baptised with the baptism of Jesus Christ, "with the Holy Spirit and with fire" (Mt 3,11). The Spirit is the source of our communion with one another, for he transcends space and time, inhabits within us, makes us transparently open to one another and enables us to relate to one another in love. It is in the unity of the Holy Spirit that, in heaven and already here on earth, to the Father, with the Son, is rendered all honour and all glory.

4. B. Rioux, *Les Mutations de la foi chrétienne* (Montreal 1974).